# THE ILLUSION OF DETERMINISM

## Why Free Will Is Real and Causal

# Edwin A. Locke

The Illusion of Determinism

Why Free Will Is Real and Causal

Edwin A. Locke

Print ISBN: 978-1-54391-422-1

eBook ISBN: 978-1-54391-423-8

Publisher: Edwin A. Locke

*To Cathy with all my love*

# CONTENTS

# ACKNOWLEDGEMENTS

I would like to thank the following people for their help and advice: Dr. Aurora LePort for her expert help on the nature of the brain; Dr. Dale Stevens for his insights into the Libet studies; Dr. Gregory Salmieri for his insightful comments on the nature of animal cognition; Dr. Evan Picoult for explaining the actual meaning of entropy; Dr. Ben Bayer for pointing to useful books on the subject of free will and certain issues in the field of philosophy; and Dr. Onkar Ghate, who made valuable comments on and suggestions for every chapter. I also want to thank Jenniffer Woodson for her outstanding job of copyediting. Finally I want to thank my dear wife, Cathy Durham, not only for her continual support but also for her help in identifying many passages that needed clarification.

No one above is responsible for any errors that may remain in the book nor for any critical oversights.

# PREFACE

The issue of free will has occupied philosophers as far back as the ancient Greeks. Plato and Aristotle were not much concerned with the concept of free will; the Stoics may have been the first to introduce the issue explicitly (Frede 2011), specifically Epictetus, who viewed free will as giving or not giving assent to your emotions. Alexander of Aphrodisias, a Peripatetic, put emphasis on the use of reason as a determinant of whether one acts on one's emotions or not.

Christian philosophers (starting with Origen in the third century and Augustine a century later) took up the issue from the Stoics, but free will did not become an official church doctrine until the fifth century. This issue caused a great deal of controversy which persists to this day. In Genesis God tells Adam and Eve not to eat the fruit of the tree of knowledge, but they disobeyed him and God banished them from the Garden of Eden. According to scripture, we have been paying the price ever since—such as being made to work for a living. To some Genesis may imply free will, but it also represents Original Sin, which is taken by some to mean that man has an innate tendency toward evil—which would imply free will but with loaded dice. There have been endless debates on the issue among Christian (and Jewish) theologians. The problem is that if God were omniscient and omnipotent, then many claim he would have to have foreknowledge of who would obey and who would sin. This would imply predestination (as in Calvinism), but this would contradict free will. Some have claimed that humans are simply unable to understand God's "higher" truths, though it is not clear by what means we could even know that he had higher truths. There can be no resolution to these contradictions in religious terms, since the whole basis for the debate (including the existence of a god), is grounded in faith and not reason.

The development of modern science added fuel to this debate. The discovery that the body was a machine which operated according to the laws of physics and chemistry (including electricity), and that consciousness depended on the existence of a brain, threatened to totally materialize man. Consciousness was dismissed by many as a mystical anachronism or as an incidental by-product of brain activity which served no function. In this view all causal relationships were mechanical. If science were to be taken seriously, then it was assumed that determinism had to be true. Thus, free will would be a myth. This view is still prevalent, though not universal. The philosophical debate has continued through the centuries within and outside of religion and is still debated today.[1] I believe that my book can help to bring about a resolution, or at least to move the debate forward. This may sound optimistic, but I think that progress has been blocked by looking at the issue too narrowly; in short, by the failure to deal with key issues that underlie the debate: the nature of consciousness, the nature of causality, the nature of goal-directed action, the locus of choice, and the failure to take the law of contradiction seriously.

Some years ago the authors of an article in a well-regarded science magazine reported the survey results of eminent evolutionary scientists (Graffin and Provine 2007, 294-97). Overwhelmingly, the scientists were not religious and equally overwhelmingly, they believed in free will. The authors were quite upset about the latter. They ended with, "Belief in free will adds nothing to the science of human behavior" (297). Unfortunately, the study did not ask the scientists to identify what they meant by free will—what it consisted of. Further, we shall see that without free will there could be no science of human behavior at all—in fact, there could be no science of anything.

---

1    See Pereboom 2009 for a sampling of the debates.

At the same time, defenders of free will have not made a convincing case. They often base free will on indeterminism (randomness), an idea taken from particle theory. This does not work. Randomness is not control.

I hope in this book to set the record straight. I must acknowledge at the outset that my key philosophical points are based on Objectivism, the philosophy of Ayn Rand, including her theory of volition. I have enlarged and expanded the discussion of the issue but am in full agreement with her views. Many of the ideas in this book are consistent with the penetrating insights of psychologist Albert Bandura. Bandura's (2008) views are his own and not based on Ayn Rand.

# INTRODUCTION

As noted in the Preface, the issue of free will vs. determinism has been debated for centuries—seemingly without resolution.

Determinism is the doctrine that everything we think, feel, believe, and do is caused by factors outside our control—that we have no choice regarding our character, our thoughts, our actions, our lives. There have been many forms of determinism but the one that is most popular today is based on neuroscience, with the enthusiastic support of many psychologists, philosophers, and physical scientists (e.g., physicists). This version argues that we are controlled by our physical brains with the brain being set in motion by environmental factors.

The debate continues because many people disagree with determinism and assert that they have, in some form, free will. Determinists insist that such a belief represents "folk psychology," an illusion held by people who are ignorant of what science has allegedly proved.

Determinists typically believe that:

- Consciousness is the same thing as brain activity (as opposed to requiring a brain)

- The conscious mind, though real, plays no significant role in human life

- The human mind is not significantly different from that of the lower animals such as chimpanzees

- All causes are material (or mechanical)

- Goal-directed action applies equally to people and machines

- The concept of a self or the self as a causal agent has no intelligible meaning

- Key neuroscience experiments have proven that the intention to act appears after the brain has already decided what to do

- Determinism is not only compatible with objective knowledge but is also the only guarantee of objective knowledge, because it is based on scientific truth

- Determinism has to be either proved or disproved based on philosophical and/or scientific arguments

- Free will, at best, is a necessary illusion

On the other side of the coin, various free will advocates typically believe that:

- Elementary particles which make up our brain act at random, thus refuting causal necessity

- Free will and determinism are compatible

- Religion validates free will

In this book I will show that *all of the above beliefs are mistaken.* I will also show that free will is, as many have claimed, self-evident, even though most people have not validated it or correctly identified what it consists of—what it is, and what it isn't.

One might ask, in relation to this dispute, why it matters. Is this merely a dispute among academics, e.g., philosophers and scientists, with no implications for the rest of us?

My view is that the implications are momentous. I will show that:

1. Without free will there could be no such thing as objective (actual) knowledge

2. Without free will there could be no such thing as morality or a moral society.

That should be incentive enough to explore this issue thoroughly.

There is another benefit to this book. Many people are not very skilled at introspection and may have been confused and/or intimidated by the onslaught of determinist arguments in books and the press. This book provides the intellectual ammunition one needs to be certain that free will is real and to know what it consists of (and does not consist of).

# 1

# THE BRAIN

This chapter is not a primer on the brain; neophytes who want details can find many books on the subject, such as *Neuroscience for Dummies*. This is simply a summary of a few basic facts (which were checked by a neuroscientist).

The brain is the hardware that makes consciousness possible and regulates (non-consciously) the functioning of one's whole body (e.g., the internal organs). Its volume is 1,400 cc. It consumes 20% of the body's metabolism or energy use. It contains between eighty-five and one hundred billion neuronal cells. Each neuron has dendrites or branches that connect to several thousand other neurons. Each dendrite contains thousands of synapses or connectors which signal each other in sequence. There are some one hundred and fifty trillion synapses in the brain. The neuron sends out signals along another type of branch called an axon, which connects the dendrites to other neurons. Signaling in the brain is done by chemicals and electricity. Experience and thinking affect the strength of the synapses. The brain also has other types of cells. For example, there are ten times one hundred billion glial cells, which support the neurons and help insure brain health, among other functions. (Note: recent research suggests that glial cells have more functions than originally thought).

The brain evolved in layers starting with more primitive vertebrates such as lizards. Depending on the organism, many brain parts have specialized functions—e.g., integrating signals from the senses, control and coordination of movement, working and long–term memory, emotion, thinking, language, planning, etc.—but nevertheless the brain is widely interconnected both within and between parts. The most recently evolved and cognitively advanced part of the brain lies atop the other regions and is called the neocortex (which itself has parts or lobes). The neocortex is unique to mammals. The human brain, mainly due to the evolved neocortex, is twice as large and somewhat differently structured compared to the neocortexes of the ape family (e.g., chimpanzees), our nearest living ancestors. This is why we have greater cognitive power than they do. The brain regions, by the way, do not act simply in sequence. Many of the parts act simultaneously, and yet the brain is still an integrated whole.

It is still a partial mystery exactly where or how consciousness originates in the brain, but research suggests that the neocortex (in concert with other brain regions) makes possible consciousness and thereby the regulation of action.

The human brain may be one of the most (if not the most) complex entities known. Considering the enormous number of cells and their high degree of specialization, the trillions of interconnections between the cells, and the massive integration among parts—all directed at protecting and enhancing life and well-being—it makes the world's largest super computers look like infants' toys by comparison. Note that computers, though extremely valuable to human civilization, are not conscious. Further, we built and programmed them; they did not build or program us.

The brain is active every second, twenty-four hours a day—even when you sleep. If brain activity ever stops, it means you are effectively dead. Nevertheless, you need more than a physical brain to survive. You need consciousness.

# 2

# WHAT IS CONSCIOUSNESS?

Consciousness is self-evident. When you look at this page, grasp the meaning of the words, and evaluate the assertions you are engaging in conscious (mental) actions. Furthermore, you know you are conscious—you are self-conscious. One would think, then, that scientists would have no problem with this concept. On the contrary, they have found it to be very upsetting. In fact, it was so upsetting to psychologists that for a period of about fifty years, the dominant view in psychology was that they should have nothing to do with it—that they should study only observable behavior, not the mind. (This bizarre doctrine was called behaviorism).[2] This rejection by psychologists of their own subject matter is analogous to the idea of physicists rejecting atoms, chemists rejecting molecules, or astronomers rejecting stars. Very odd, indeed. Most physical scientists, especially neuroscientists, have been no more sympathetic to consciousness than many old time behaviorists, and even today many psychologists are in sympathy with the neuroscientists' view. Some neuroscientists claim to be baffled about why consciousness evolved at all.

---

2    The most famous advocate of behaviorism was B. F. Skinner. His most famous popular book was *Beyond Freedom and Dignity* 1971. For a trenchant critique of this book and various commentaries on it, see Ayn Rand's 1972 article "The Stimulus...and the Response."

## Mind and Brain

What has been the problem? It is this: *consciousness is just not like other stuff*. Many scientists find the concept of consciousness to be baffling and ultimately unacceptable because their whole scientific world view is based on material objects and mechanical causation. Some deny consciousness completely, claiming mind and brain are the same thing. This is called the *psycho-neural identity theory* (sometimes called extreme reductionism or materialism). But this claim is self-evidently false. We easily distinguish mind from matter; being aware of an object is different from being the object. To say that we are aware of a chair presupposes that the two are different. It would not make any sense to say that my mind is a chair. (A claim of identity here would be a sign of mental illness.) To carry the analysis a step further, it is obvious that mind and matter have different attributes. For example, physical objects can be large or square or heavy or green, but conscious thoughts have neither size nor shape nor weight nor color. In contrast, conscious thoughts can be logical, clear, abstract, conflicted, or confused. Physical objects have none of these attributes. (Elementary particles may have different attributes than observable objects, e.g., spin, but these attributes do not pertain to ideas either). *Since an existent is the sum or integration of its attributes, matter and consciousness cannot be the same thing.* (Note: attributes do not exist separately from an entity. A ten foot, square, green, plastic cube weighing 1,000 pounds is just that—there is no ineffable "substratum" underlying these characteristics.)

Others have argued for a slightly different view: that neural connections and thoughts are two different aspects of the same underlying physical existent (the brain). This is called the *dual or double aspect theory*, but the same problem remains. Since there is no overlap in attributes, there can be no underlying existent that has the attributes of both mind and matter. When you introspect, you do not see neurons—and when surgeons visually inspect brain tissue they do not see ideas. Try to imagine this preposterous, dual aspect example: a house that is yellow and square on one side and suffers from anxiety and psychological conflict on the other side! Of course you can't imagine this at all, except as science fiction. In reality, the dual aspect theory is simply unintelligible. (Diehards may claim that new discoveries will somehow solve the problem, but a hope is not a fact.)

A third and the most commonly held view is that, "Okay, consciousness exists and is different than other stuff, but it doesn't do anything." This view is called *epiphenomenalism*; consciousness is seen as an incidental by-product of brain activity. Consider this analogy: when you drop a plate and break it, there is a sound. But the sound did not cause the break; it was a by-product of it. Epiphenomenalists see consciousness in the same way. To the determinist, the idea that consciousness can cause anything smacks of mysticism or supernaturalism. But in reality, we know that consciousness makes a difference; you could not survive and guide action if you were always sleeping or in a coma. When you are awake, you can perceive things and think and that makes a difference; it affects what you do. (The insuperable contradiction inherent in epiphenomenalism and all forms of determinism will be discussed in Chapter Seven.)[3]

There is another view of the relation of mind and brain called *dualism*. (This view is mainly due to philosopher Rene Descartes.) In one variant consciousness is ineffable or supernatural and thus beyond science. A related view is that it is a separate, somewhat mysterious substance within the body that has no connection with the brain, though it can upon occasion come into contact with it. Dualism in either variant is usually associated with religion. Consciousness, however, is not supernatural; it is a natural faculty of certain living organisms. There is not the slightest evidence that consciousness, in the form of a disembodied soul, traipses around the earth or the universe when we die. There can be no rational

---

3    A popular psychologist-champion of epiphenomenalism was the late Daniel Wegner, author of *The Illusion of Popular Will* 1979. His theme was that because people can be mistaken about what they can control or about what they conclude about control from introspection, therefore they are mistaken about thinking they can control anything. The book is a massive non-sequitur.

doubt that consciousness depends on the existence of an organism with sense organs and a brain. As noted in Chapter One, the brain is a physical organ which functions by means of electricity and chemicals. When the brain dies, what it makes possible—consciousness—dies with it. *Divorcing consciousness from an actual living entity contradicts everything we know about the nature of life, the brain, and the mind.*

What then is the relationship of mind to brain? *I believe the most logical way to look at it is to view consciousness as an emergent faculty or power made possible by a certain type of biological structure.* (I will have more to say about emergent faculties in later chapters.)[4] To summarize, consciousness is made possible by and dependent upon the existence of a functioning brain (as part of a human or animal which has sense organs and a nervous system); but, as noted, it is not the same thing as, or not identical to, a brain. My view is the same idea as what some call property dualism. I prefer not to use the term dualism, due to how it has been used and abused in the past.

## Consciousness as Axiomatic

What then is the philosophical or conceptual status of consciousness? Here we run into another issue that has bedeviled scientists and philosophers: *consciousness cannot be defined.* That is, consciousness has no genus or differentia (such as: man is the rational animal). *This is because consciousness is a self-evident primary.* It has a rough synonym, awareness, but that is just another word for the same thing. The experience of awareness cannot be derived or deduced from anything else. It is sui generis (unique). You experience it directly and can explain it to another, say a child, only ostensively, by pointing to an example: "Do you see that table? That means you are conscious of it." "Do you hear that tune? That means you are conscious of it." You cannot go deeper—only offer more examples.

---

4    Michael Gazzaniga, author of *Who's in Charge?: Free Will and the Science of the Brain* 2011, agrees with the idea of emergence, although his approach to the free will issue is different from the one in this book.

(It should be possible someday to fully identify the neural basis of consciousness—see Chapter One for some things that we know now—but that still would not be a definition.)[5]

Philosophically (and scientifically) *consciousness is an axiom*: it is a self-evident starting point for all knowledge and it cannot be negated without using it in the process. Claiming that "I know I am not conscious" is a contradiction (Rand 1990). But it is not the primary axiom, contrary to Descartes. Existence comes first. Descartes' error was to make consciousness a primary: "I think, therefore I am." Rand's formulation was the opposite: "I am, therefore I think." To quote Rand (1990):

> Existence exists—and the act of grasping that statement implies two corollary axioms: that something exists which one perceives and that one exists possessing consciousness, consciousness being the faculty of perceiving that which exists.
>
> If nothing exists there can be no consciousness: a consciousness conscious of nothing but itself is a contradiction in terms: before it could identify itself as consciousness it had to be conscious of something (quoted in Binswanger 1986, 92).

Given that one is conscious of something, one can, through introspection, identify one's thoughts and cognitive processes. But existence is the primary axiom (existence exists). A third axiom, the law of identity, will be discussed in the next chapter.

Philosophers often use the term "intentionality" to refer to the fact that conscious ideas represent something outside the mind, e.g., objects in the world. However, this term is simply not necessary. It is quite sufficient to say that *to be conscious is to be conscious of something* (Rand 1990). The term intentionality only leads to unnecessary confusion. Given that one

---

5    Nobel Laureate Gerald Edelman and co-author Giulio Tononi 2000 seem to understand that consciousness is something made possible by the brain, but different from it—and that it has causal efficacy.

is conscious of something, one can, through introspection, then identify one's thoughts and cognitive processes.

Some skeptic philosophers (especially Immanuel Kant) have argued that the real world, existence, is unknowable. All we can actually know, they say, is appearances (the contents of our consciousness).[6] One has to ask: how could they even know that there is a world out there if it is unknowable? An appearance is the appearance of something. Of course, there is a big element of hypocrisy in skepticism, because it could not be used as a real guide to action. When skeptics cross the street, they are looking out for an actual car coming. The appearance of a car would not hurt them; a real car would kill them if they did not stay out of the way and they know it. When they check their bank balance, they are interested in the actual amount of money they have, not its appearance inside their heads. If they get sick they want to be treated by an actual doctor, not the appearance of a doctor in their minds. As per the Ayn Rand quote above, it is by means of consciousness, starting with the sense organs, that we come to know reality.

It is sometimes asked whether consciousness is a potential, a state, or a process. Actually, it is all three. As a potential it refers to the fact that one can be aware of something in the world (or in one's memory), even if one is not aware of it at the moment (or not aware of it at all, as in sleep). As a state it refers to what one perceives or feels or thinks at a given time. As a process it refers to the fact that consciousness is active. Consciousness is both a differentiating and an integrating mechanism (Rand 1990). It discriminates among existents and can group them together (to varying degrees) based on similarity. Consciousness has identity. This brings us to the two basic levels of consciousness. (I will skip any discussion of sensations, since there is debate as to whether the concept is useful for understanding perception.)

---

6    For critiques of Kant's philosophy, see Ayn Rand, *For the New Intellectual* 1961; Leonard Peikoff, *The DIM Hypothesis* 2012; and Onkar Ghate, "Postmodernism's Kantian Roots," in Edwin A. Locke's *Postmodernism in Management: Pros, Cons and the Alternative* 2003. For key excerpts from Kant, see Harry Binswanger, *Ayn Rand Lexicon* 1986.

## Levels of Consciousness

*Perception.* Man shares with the higher animals the perceptual awareness of existence. The sense organs function automatically and non-consciously to receive and integrate incoming stimuli and thereby give us awareness of objects and the attributes and actions of objects (i.e., their size, shape, color, motion, etc.). This capacity is critical to survival. Let's start with the higher animals. Perception, along with a built-in plea-sure-pain mechanism, guides locomotion toward beneficial objects and away from harmful objects. Animals, like people, can retain information in the form of memory. This means that they can learn from experience and retain perceptual associations. (To put words they do not have into their mouths: X is the place where there is food and water; Y is the place where there are dangerous creatures.) For animals, the perceptual level of functioning (along with their bodily mechanisms) is usually sufficient for survival if the environment to which they have adapted does not change too rapidly or too drastically. Man shares these capacities with animals, but is able to go—and needs to go—one step further, because man cannot sur-vive at the perceptual level alone. Animals have more acute sense organs and are often stronger or faster, or can find and digest foods that humans cannot. (See Chapter Four for further discussion.)

*Conceptualization.* Many scholars claim to be baffled by the ques-tion: what makes humans exceptional? The answer is: the rational faculty, the ability to conceptualize. This was a giant step in evolution, although there were evidently many intermediate species between the apes and modern humans across a period of perhaps six million years. Of course, the intermediate species between apes and modern man became extinct. What does the conceptual or rational level involve? How do concepts get formed? Humans form concepts by looking at similarities and differences between objects and integrating them in a way that animals cannot. For example, they can observe among plane figures that some have more sides than others. Those with three sides they can group together—mentally integrate—omitting differences in size, place, color, location, and the arrangement of the angles. They treat all three-sided plane figures as a single mental unit and label the concept with a name: triangle. They can define the concept: a triangle is plane figure bounded by three straight lines. The specific angles (which must sum to one hundred and eighty degrees) and sizes are omitted; they must exist in some quantity but the concept does not specify them. The definition is a way of keeping one's concepts clear and differentiated, as in a file folder, but the definition is not the same as the concept. The concept of triangle encompasses everything known about triangles (e.g., the different types, the relationships among the sides and the angles, etc.), including things not yet discovered about them.[7] The concept can encompass an unlimited number of objects with the relevant attributes.

Similarly, consider mathematics. Humans are able to separate by abstraction number (quantity) from specific objects. Ten or ten thousand can be ten or ten thousand of anything (dollars, donuts, or daisies). The content is left unspecified. Observe that the concept of number is the foundation of the science of mathematics, with millions of applications to every aspect of human life. Consider how many features of our civilization depend on this one capability. The concept of number is only one of many thousands of concepts that men grasp and use every day. Dictionaries in any given language consist of thousands of pages of concepts.

What's the benefit of having and using concepts? Unit economy (Rand 1990). A single concept, designated by a single word, means it is a single unit in the mind that can stand for an unlimited number of concretes or attributes of a certain type.

The ability to conceptualize, when fully developed, allowed human civilization to explode, especially over the last 2,000 years. Consider the many millions of discoveries and inventions that have made it possible for humans to flourish. The internet might be viewed as, in essence, the sum of

---

7   See Ayn Rand's *Introduction to Objectivist Epistemology 1990* for a detailed explanation of her theory of concepts.

all human knowledge. Estimates vary but it may contain as many as forty billion web pages.

Despite the directly observable fact that humans have created great civilizations while apes are still living in the jungle, some psychologists insist that man and chimp are really not that different—that any differences one observes are only a matter of degree. The claims include, for example, that in some form animals can grasp concepts, use tools, and solve problems just like us. Such claims require massive equivocations, to put it politely.

Let's begin with the fact that animals cannot count. Many animal species and humans can perceptually discriminate, without using labels, one object from two, three from four, and five from six: up to about six from seven. Above about seven, perception does not do the trick. To discriminate, say, ten from eleven, you have to count, which means you have to grasp the concept of number divorced from objects. Animals cannot do this. Some psychologists argue that animals can discriminate "numerosity," that is, the ability to discriminate a larger from a smaller numbers of objects. But the only way they could do this is to discriminate differences in perceptual density. They could not do it by counting. The entire field of mathematics is beyond their capability.

What about tools? Psychologists claim that animals are like us because they use tools. But what are their tools? Natural objects like twigs, straws, and rocks. What do these tools have in common with electric drills, medical devices, cars, airplanes, computers, cell phones, and the complex machinery used to run factories? The "tools" used by animals have, in fact, nothing in common with the tools used in human civilizations. Such a massive technological gap cannot be covered up by using the same word for both types of objects. It would be like saying that a squirrel burying a nut and a person designing a retirement plan are both investing. Human tools require conceptual thinking: e.g., the discovery of metals, electricity, and mathematical measurement plus forethought regarding how to make ncluding integrating the parts) and what they will be used for e (which may involve days, weeks, months, or years). Animal ιools" require only sense perception and trial and error.

Psychologists have trumpeted the alleged ability of animals to grasp concepts and thereby solve problems. But the tricks that animals are able to learn are things taught to them by psychologists. Psychologists use *this* trick to make people believe animals can grasp concepts: they reduce the concepts to percepts, or simple, concrete actions. For example, teaching chimps "hurt" reduces to teaching them to respond to a red streak on someone's skin; teaching "language" reduces to training a chimp to emit random strings of symbols, some of which might get them food.[8]

These actions only require sense perception, memory, and reward— chimps can learn to press buttons on a computer screen to get food. These are tricks they couldn't have learned on their own; nor could they invent psychological laboratories or computers. More complex animal activities are chains of actions under the control of perceptions, desires, and some innate mechanisms.

At the deepest level, consider the most obvious fact of all: in the six million years since primitive man broke off from the apes, chimpanzees (or bonobos, if you like), the species most similar to us in DNA, have achieved nothing at all culturally. There was no ascent from the swamps to the stars; there was no ascent to anything. Animals cannot get past the perceptual level. They cannot even solve the problem of their own survival as humans encroach on their territories; it will require interested humans to save them. But they can do nothing to save us.

This is not to deny that animals can perceptually discriminate the shapes of objects. Animals can detect perceptual similarities and differ- ences—certain objects look alike or different than other objects. They can

---

8    See Herb Terrace's *Nim* 1979 for an expose of the alleged ability of chimps to grasp language; he found that word sounds functioned as (often randomly emitted) perceptual signals rather than conceptual integrations. Terrace does believe apes have a self concept but see Chapter Five of this book.

make perceptual groupings. Wildebeests that could not distinguish lions from zebras would be hard put to survive on the African plains. If they ran from every animal they saw, they would die of exhaustion or starvation; if they ran from none, they would be eaten. But such discriminations do not mean that animals view a specific lion as part of a cognitive unit (concept) named "lion." Rather, seeing a lion calls up memories of similar entities. In the same way, pet dogs can see that people look alike and are different than trees. If it could talk, the dog might say "that looks like a thing that feeds me." But a dog cannot form the concept of man (the rational animal), a very wide abstraction (Rand 1990).

Many scientists claim that it is language that separates man and animal. This is true, but it is not the most fundamental point. Language (other than proper nouns) consists of words that stand for concepts. Language is more than just perceptual (i.e., auditory) signals such as used by birds or porpoises; or frantic strings of sounds put together arbitrarily (Terrace 1979). It's conceptualization that makes language possible (Rand 1990). Neuroscientists usually don't get this and probably for this reason: words (combinations of letters) in themselves are entities and are directly perceivable, just like chairs and tables. Perception is a non-conscious brain activity (though it ends in awareness). This means that the neuroscientist can pretend to treat a word like an object, divorced from its conceptual meaning. On the other hand, concepts, the basis for language, are cognitive integrations, i.e., abstractions or mental entities (Rand 1990) that have no attributes in common with physical matter, including brain matter—even though the brain makes conceptualization possible.[9]

---

9    It is striking that those (other than Rand) who write about the mind and/or the brain virtually never identify conceptualization, i.e., reasoning, as the distinctive feature of man and how it differs from perception. One book used the terms "consciousness 1" and "consciousness 2," evidently to distinguish perception from conception, but without any definitions. Another claimed that the key difference between man and animal is helping, but helping in the human sense is a consequence of being conceptual. (Some animals can help one another in a very limited way). Another writer says the key feature of the human level of consciousness is explicitness, but does not explain what this means.

*Error and volition.* Aside from forming concepts as such, two aspects of functioning at the conceptual level (in contrast to the perceptual level) need to be identified. First, conceptual conclusions can be wrong. In the case of perception itself, it is beyond evaluation qua perception. Perceptual information is a given—it can't even be called right or wrong in the conceptual sense, though percepts can be analyzed conceptually. The sense organs send signals to the brain which automatically integrates them and gives awareness of some object or an attribute of an object. You can't argue that perception is invalid without a contradiction: how would you know there is a so-called perceptual error except by perception? Consider looking down railroad tracks. They appear to converge in the distance, but we know they don't actually converge, because we can walk down the tracks and see that they are parallel. The appearance of convergence is due to our visual system automatically integrating size and distance—things look smaller when they are far away. Or consider that a pencil looks crooked in water because the water refracts light waves differently than air. We can see that the pencil is not bent by removing it from the water and also feeling it. The bent shape is how a pencil looks in water (though it does not feel bent in water, because light waves play no role here). Conceptually we can misinterpret perceptions; for example, a child seeing train tracks for the first time might conclude that the tracks actually come together because it "looks like" they do. But they can readily learn the truth, because they learn early in life, through vision and locomotion, about the relation of perception and distance. When they go to the top of the Empire State building and look down, they may say at first: "Wow, look at the tiny people on the street." But they will readily learn that this is caused by the long distance. To see bodily features and proportions from such a distance, one would have to use binoculars.

Some philosophers and scientists argue against the validity of perception because the information is processed—implying that true reality could only be known if the material were not processed—perception by no specific means. This is impossible. *It is only because we have a means of awareness that we can know things* (Ghate 2003, Rand 1990).

In contrast to percepts, conceptual conclusions have to be validated. If two sets of two blocks rest on a table, perceptually one will see them. But one may conclude mathematically, and falsely, that two and two are five. Or, going farther afield, consider falsehoods such as that cholera is caused by bad air; that heavier than air objects cannot fly; or that people lacking aristocratic blood or having black skin have no rights. Conceptual conclusions need to be validated by a certain method. This is why the science of epistemology is needed. We need to know how to know and how to know that we know (Peikoff 1991).

This book is not a treatise on epistemology, but I will make several sub-points. First, a key aspect of the validation of conceptual knowledge is reduction, or tracing back our conclusions to the perceptual level which is the base of all knowledge. This keeps our concepts tied to reality. Second, we must respect the law of contradiction. This law (from Aristotle) says that a thing cannot be A and non-A at the same time and in the same respect. If there is a contradiction between X and Y, both cannot be true, although both can be false. This law is a law of logic because it is a law of reality. (Two and two equals four is not just a linguistic rule; when you manage your money, you will see that bad things happen if you spend more than you can afford by pretending two and two make four thousand.) Third, conceptualization requires induction: observing facts and integrating them with each other and with all of one's other knowledge.[10] The second way that the conceptual level differs from the perceptual is that the conceptual level does not function automatically. The brain does not automatically create valid

---

10    Here is an example of deliberate non-integration: when psychologists claim that they have done experiments showing that animals can think just like us, they evade the fact that no animal species has ever built even the rudiments of a culture or a civilization—or a laboratory filled with equipment developed and operated by psychologists who do experiments and write articles.

concepts, definitions, propositions, scientific laws, or moral principles. The history of the world shows how many wrong conclusions people have reached on every subject, along with the many valid discoveries that have moved civilization forward. The road from the swamps to the stars was filled with millions of dead ends, together with earth-shaking discoveries (such as the Greeks' discovery of philosophy, Newton's laws of motion, and Darwin's theory of evolution). As we will see later in this book, free will is intimately connected to the conceptual level of functioning.

Unlike the case of perception, which is automatic, conceptualizing and everything associated with it—e.g., reasoning, planning, projecting, integrating, problem solving, inducing, deducing, etc.—requires mental effort. People can choose not to exert mental effort, typically with unfortunate and often disastrous consequences. Here is one example: many people do not plan for retirement and become impoverished and traumatized as they age. Without the guidance of conscious purpose, one's life simply goes out of control and reduces to "chance" (i.e., unplanned associations).

## The Conscious and the Subconscious

Defined broadly, consciousness as a state is what is in awareness now, but as a faculty it also includes what can be brought into awareness from the subconscious. The subconscious can be thought of as storage (or memory). *The subconscious is potential awareness.* It does not imply or require a homunculus, a little person inside your head making decisions. Subconscious material is just information waiting to be consciously accessed. Very little of what is in consciousness is actually in awareness at any given moment. We can only hold about seven disconnected items in awareness simultaneously. The same is true for animals. (Ayn Rand calls this the "crow epistemology" referring to the fact that crows can allegedly distinguish between five and say seven hunters going into the woods and leaving but cannot distinguish five from ten because they cannot count). What is not in focal awareness goes into storage, which involves trillions of connections. As noted in Chapter One, the storage capacity of the brain is enormous. It is not true that every experience you have ever had is recorded in the brain, but much of it is. Validating the concept of the subconscious is simple: if you are asked: "Tell me about your mother," and you choose to answer, the needed material comes to awareness automatically, by some form of association, with no need for any new learning. The subconscious is not the same as the unconscious or the non-conscious. For example, the mechanisms governing your sense perceptions are non-conscious: they cannot be brought into awareness. You are only aware of the results. As to the issue of one's ability to bring up strongly repressed memories that are unconscious (as in Freudian psychology), I leave that to others to study.

Repressed memories aside, how does it all work? We start with being conscious. Sense perception is the base of all our knowledge (Rand 1990). What we experience gets stored in the subconscious. Through repetition what we learn through perception gets automatized along with the things we learn conceptually. For example, as we acquire language, the meanings of all the words we know and the rules of grammar and sentence construction get stored. Some of this happens automatically, though as the concepts become more complex, we have to do hard mental work to program material into our memory (e.g., the definition of words, grammar, arithmetic, algebra, etc.). That's why children need to be educated. Developing conceptual knowledge and skill (e.g., language skills) requires thousands of hours of focused effort and practice. The same is true for many physical skills (e.g., playing a musical instrument). For people who choose to remain purposeful, learning continues throughout life.

How does the subconscious material arise when stored? By association based on learning and experience. The process can be started simply by observing something, such as a known object or person. The process can also be initiated by a conscious purpose. For example, if we choose to engage in a conversation, all of our grammar and word knowledge comes into play automatically—we don't have to look up every spoken word we hear. If we had to do this, we could hardly converse at all. Our conscious mind is then left free to focus on the meaning of what the other person is saying—that is, how the words combine to express a thought or idea. This cannot be fully automatized, because you have to listen and the number of possible combinations and arrangements of words is virtually unlimited. If we decide to ride a bike, we do not have to learn to ride all over again. It all comes back through "muscle memory" when we get on the bike, but we still have to look where we are going. If we are solving a problem, we call up knowledge that we think is relevant, but we may also have to make new connections, since not all problems are routine.

Neuroscientists like to negate the conscious mind by claiming that everything the conscious mind does can be done by the subconscious. Such a claim requires a good deal of evasion. To start with the most obvious fact: if there were no conscious mind there would be nothing to store in the subconscious at all. The conscious mind, through the senses, encounters new facts every day. People do no learn when they are unconscious. If people were chronically unaware of reality, they could not survive except in an institution. People learn new things every day which are stored and then called into awareness when relevant to a purpose. When we decide to drive somewhere, we rely on skills previously automatized—but at the same time we have to be aware of the traffic, which differs every day on every road. We need to pay full attention even as we use automatized skills. If we are not paying conscious attention and making choices, we are very likely to get into an accident. This is why texting while driving is so dangerous (if your car is not self-driving).

The conscious mind functions as a director/orchestrator in life. Consider your relationship with Amazon.com as a metaphor. Its warehouses store millions of products. How do you get what you want? By placing an order based on your purpose (e.g., to buy a certain book). The ordered object then comes to you "automatically," without further thought or action on your part.

The conscious mind can manage the process because it is active, whereas the subconscious is fundamentally passive. As noted, like the Amazon warehouse, it is storage. It follows orders. One can consciously give the subconscious a standing order such as "think about this" and it may come up with something. There is debate about whether the subconscious does some integrating on its own, divorced from conscious orders. This is not of concern here. We know that the brain is always active as long as you are alive (Chapter One). If the conscious mind goes passive by choice, the subconscious feeds the conscious mind something from storage on its own (daydreaming).

There is another point to be made about orchestration: *purposeful regulation keeps out what is irrelevant to one's purpose by focusing the mind selectively.* Given the enormous amount of material stored in the subconscious, everything cannot come out at once. If it did, it would destroy the conscious mind. It is fortunate for us that the conscious mind can only focus on a limited number of things at the same time.

Determinists who disparage the role of the conscious mind in life are trying to defend an idea which would lead to death—living unconsciously. And they are denying what is self-evident in their own lives on an everyday basis. They have to be conscious about what they are doing (at least some of the time).[11]

There is a final point to made here: *successful living always requires the functioning of both the conscious and the subconscious.* Without the conscious mind, one could not be in contact with reality or learn or act purposefully, and without the subconscious one could not retain anything

---

11   Gazzaniga 2011 belittles the conscious mind for being slow. It is true that the subconscious works at lightning speed, but the conscious mind is not exactly a slowpoke. Simple reaction time can be as fast as one twentieth of a second. Gazzaniga gives a personal example of avoiding a snake in the grass, arguing that the reaction is too fast to be based on awareness; but this is misleading. The subconscious is not in contact with reality so there would have to be some peripheral awareness for any reaction to take place, even if the reaction was faster than one's ability to label the object or put it into words.

(acquire knowledge). Lose either one and the human race disappears from the earth. The claim by some neuroscientists that the conscious mind has no real function is too bizarre to be taken seriously. One wonders what faculty they used to come to such a conscious conclusion.

In everyday life there is a constant interplay between the conscious and the subconscious. There is constant trafficking between the two, as per the examples of engaging in a conversation or driving noted earlier. Your conscious purpose, if you have one, still directs the process but the subconscious processing is ongoing—and necessary.

It is true that things in the environment may call up certain associations in the absence of a conscious purpose. For example, you may see an advertisement for ice cream in the paper and this leads you to think of buying ice cream. But this will occur only if ice cream is a value. If not, the ad will be ignored. You may be trying to lose weight. You may have more important priorities. Most people are deluged with thousands of "stimuli" all day long, but they could not possibly act on all of them even if they wanted to. *Conscious purposes prime the subconscious.*

The subconscious can also be primed with minimal conscious focus, but that cannot direct long-term, purposeful action. You can act without thinking. If the conscious mind is passive (you are not putting forth purposeful mental effort), the subconscious can "take over" both mental content and action by default, meaning that you will be acting on impulse. There can, of course, be conflicts between conscious and subconscious values; a person not fully committed to losing weight can be tempted by sweets. Giving into temptation repeatedly means that you still want what you do not think you should do. Over time such habits can become heavily automatized and specific procedures are required to change them (Locke and Dennis 2012).

A word is in order about emotions. Emotions are automatic processes based on subconscious value appraisals (Locke 2009). One experiences them but the causes can be identified only if one introspects backwards and identifies them. One has to be conscious to name the emotion and also to change it (by re-programming the subconscious.) There is also rumination: replaying events and their accompanying emotions over and over. This can happen because there are unresolved issues involved or because one's brain is wired physically in a way that makes inhibition difficult. (More on this in Chapter Eight.)

This brings us to the next issue: how exactly does life depend on the mind, including the conscious mind?

## Reason and Survival

Some years ago in a doctoral seminar I was discussing the functioning of the conceptual, i.e., rational, mind and at one point I said, thinking it was self-evident: "Of course you all know the connection between reason and survival, right?" Wrong; no one did. My mistake.

I am going to take food as an example, given that food is a life and death matter. Animals in the wild find food in nature, consisting of other animals, fruits, berries, nuts, leaves, grass, etc. Their perceptual mechanism, memory, learning, the pleasure-pain mechanism, and locomotion guided by the senses work together; survival in most cases is a day to day or week to week matter.

Early man (e.g., *Homo habilis*) learned to hunt in coordinated groups and to make primitive garments, tools, and weapons—perhaps signaling the beginnings of conceptual thought. They were hunter-gatherers who lived off what nature provided. Modern man, *Homo sapiens sapiens*, dates back about 200,000 years and is the only surviving hominid species.[12]

Two major steps in cultural development, starting about 10,000 to 12,000 years ago, were the domestication of animals and agriculture (farming); these are unheard of in the animal kingdom and in hunter-gatherer

---

12   There are a small number of very primitive, isolated tribes living in certain parts of the world, e.g., Brazil. These may belong to a less developed hominid species.

societies. What was the key advance made possible by farming? *It was the ability of people to create and store their own food rather than trying to find it in nature.* Consider what the development of farming required conceptually. These early men had to discover plants that produced something nourishing and edible. They had to discover seeds and that seeds grew into plants. They had to figure out what soils were suitable for planting which crops. They had to figure out how to plant the seeds and make them flourish, i.e., by fertilizing and watering them. They eventually developed complex irrigation systems. They had to learn when to plant and to harvest. They had to learn how to process what they grew (e.g., to make flour). They had to learn what could be stored and by what means and for how long. They developed systems for trading for food (and other objects) which required record keeping and counting. The ability to grow food in abundance (climate permitting) through conscious intent and planning enabled early civilizations to expand and flourish for hundreds of years (e.g., the Romans and the Greeks).

Food production has now progressed to levels unthinkable to early agrarian societies, due to advances in science and technology involving extraordinary, complex intellectual achievements—including genetic engineering, fertilization, food storage, refrigeration, canning, transportation, and safety. In 10,000 BCE the estimated world's population was about four million. We can now feed most of the world's population of over seven billion people. Every one of these discoveries required conceptual thinking, which included the ability to plan long range.[13]

I have only discussed food. It should not be necessary to discuss the obvious role of reason in making earth-shaking developments in philosophy possible, especially the Greeks' identification of the nature and function of reason. This paved the way for progress in the sciences (including

---

13  Some factors causing ancient civilizations to collapse included: lack of food and water due to drought, not to mention disease, internal conflict, war, and natural disasters.

medicine) and technology, which has allowed human civilizations to grow and prosper.[14]

It should not be concluded from this that survival only concerns discoveries about nature, i.e., knowledge acquisition. Everything one encounters, thinks about, or discovers is evaluated automatically and sub-consciously and experienced in the form of emotions. But life requires conscious evaluation, too; emotions may not give correct evaluations. People need to answer the question: is this good for me or bad for me? Both knowledge and evaluation are needed to guide action.

Given the need for values, how did civilizations insure that people within a society could live together peacefully? All of them had to develop a code of behavior or code of laws that regulated what people were allowed to do (e.g., trade, according to certain rules) and not do (e. g., steal or kill). It required extensive conceptual thought to identify principles of conduct for society.

This does not mean that the laws were always just; they could be cruel and arbitrary but at least they were usually known in advance. For thousands of years it was assumed that groups (tribes, cities, races) that were not yours were ripe for destruction or enslavement. It was not until the seventeenth century that the concept of individual rights was formulated. This was another extraordinary intellectual achievement that took centuries of thought to come to fruition—starting with the ancient Greeks, reaching (partial) culmination in John Locke's *Second Treatise on Government* in 1689, and first implemented by the United States of America.[15]

Unfortunately, many countries have never accepted the concept of rights (or the virtue of reason); the bloodbaths instigated by Nazis and Communists led to over one hundred million deaths. The world is still populated by many dictators and religions that think nothing of torturing,

---

14    For documentation of Aristotle's philosophy in the achievements of western civilization (much more than Plato's), see Herman 2014 and Rand 1961.
15    Locke's treatment was not without flaws; see Ayn Rand's full validation of the concept of individual rights in Peikoff 1991.

imprisoning, or murdering thousands or millions simply to keep or extend their power. Like food, the concept of rights is a life or death issue that has to be discovered and validated—the concept is not built into our genes nor into our perceptions. And the principle has to be applied. In the U.S. it took a civil war to end slavery.

Based on knowledge and values, one's consciousness functions to guide action. Survival requires that one do something, that one pursue values in the real world. To guide successful action requires the senses plus thought (reasoning, planning, anticipation, goal setting, self-assessment, invention) and evaluation. So much for the connection between consciousness (reason, conceptualization) and life. Let the determinists explain the development of human civilization while claiming that men are solely material entities controlled by mechanical forces or by the subconscious, and that rational, conceptual thought is irrelevant to life.

One commentator said that it was possible to imagine a world of unconscious zombies living normal lives. One could imagine such creatures (Hollywood loves to do this), but one could not rationally imagine them surviving for more than a week, if that long.

As to those who claim that consciousness is only for emergencies, not using it would make one's whole life a permanent emergency—and a very short-lived one.

## Summary

Since this is a long and complex chapter, a summary of the essential points is in order. Consciousness is a philosophical and scientific axiom. It requires a brain. It is real but not material. It is our means of knowing reality (though existence is the primary axiom). The conceptual (rational) faculty builds on the material provided by the senses. Consciousness as a faculty includes the conscious mind and material stored in the subconscious, which can become conscious. Both aspects work together, with the conscious mind being active and the subconscious relatively passive.

Reason is fallible and requires an epistemology and the choice to expend effort. Consciousness is our main means of survival and of human progress.

# 3

# CAUSALITY

For many years the concept of causality was held in disrepute by philosophers, thanks to an influential skeptic named David Hume (1711-1776). He argued that one could perceive spatial and temporal contiguity between one event and another but not actual causality—that is, necessary connections. Following Hume, another philosopher, Immanuel Kant (1724-1804), agreed that causality could not be observed but asserted that it was a category built into the human mind which imposed causal perceptions on our experiences. Both agreed that you could not observe or discover actual causality based on observations of the outside world.

What's wrong with these views?

Let us consider how we come to grasp causality philosophically. It starts with the axiom noted earlier: existence exists—i.e., reality is real (Rand 1990). Contrary to Kant, reality is knowable by means of consciousness (the second axiom), starting with our senses.[16] What do we first perceive in reality? Entities. Every entity is something specific, that is, it has specific attributes or characteristics. This is the third axiom, *the law of identity*. Only particulars exist (as Aristotle pointed out). Every entity has a nature; to be is to be something. An entity that is nothing in particular is

---

16  For a refutation of Kant's core argument (that because we have a specific means of perceiving reality, we cannot perceive it), see Ghate 2003.

nothing. Nothing is not a different form of existence; nothing means: no thing. The axiom of identity is implicit in (a corollary of) the axiom of existence (Peikoff 1991). To put it simply: everything is something.

An entity's attributes and characteristics determine what it can do or will do in any specific circumstance. Every entity has specific capacities or potentialities. "Causality is the law of identity applied to action" (Binswanger 1986; for this and other relevant quotes from Ayn Rand on causality). It is critical to note that *causes are entities, not disembodied actions.* A cause is a thing acting. Every action is the action of something. For example, there are many different compounds composed of carbon and hydrogen atoms; each has a different arrangement of atoms giving each a unique identity, e.g., gas, liquid, solid, polymer—with many variations within each (Gray 2014). Each compound has a unique capacity for action.

Given that the law of identity is an axiom and thus universal, causality must be universal. If a thing is what it is, it can only act in accordance with its nature. (This is fully compatible with volition, as we shall see in Chapter Eight.) Paper burns when exposed to flame; ice melts under the same condition. Plants grow when exposed to $CO_2$ and sunlight; rocks do not. Hydrogen and oxygen combine to make water; helium and lithium do not. Acorns grow into oak trees but not into petunias. Fertilized human eggs produce babies, not cell phones. As to elementary particles, we may not now be able to measure or predict, given our present knowledge, the speed and position of single elementary particles at the same time, but this does not mean that they have neither. Particles (atoms, electrons, etc.) cannot act randomly. Particles do not "spontaneously" turn into hot fudge sundaes or become airplanes—not rarely, not ever. We know that elementary particles in the aggregate follow mathematical laws, which would be impossible if single particles acted randomly (Hawking 1996).

Causality as such applies to both inanimate matter and living organisms. Consciousness is an attribute of certain living organisms and has a nature. Animals approach prey and avoid predators guided by conscious desires and perceptions. Human beings use the senses plus reason to gain knowledge and to guide their choices and actions (see Chapter Two and other chapters to follow.)

Given the law of identity, *there can be nothing random in the universe.* To what then does the term randomness refer? *Randomness is an epistemological concept—it pertains to our lack of knowledge, not to a lack of causality. When we have partial knowledge, we can make estimates of probability.*

Some free will defenders argue for "probabilistic causation" but metaphysically (in reality) there is no such thing. There can only be probabilistic prediction based on partial knowledge. Your chance of winning the Reader's Digest sweepstakes is one in about thirty million; your chance of dying in a commercial plane crash in a first world country is one in ten million; your chance of dying of heart disease or stroke is one in three (varying by age, lifestyle, gender, and other factors); your chance of flipping a coin that will come up heads is one out of two. Probabilistic laws in science, such as radioactive decay (e.g., the half-life of radium is 1,600 years), which allow for prediction, could never be formulated and would never hold up unless the particles as a group behaved in a lawful fashion. Imagine that radioactive decay were actually random. The half-life of a specific radioactive substance as measured today might be three minutes, tomorrow 3,000 years and the next day three million years. All would be chaos; science would collapse.

Some claim there is metaphysical randomness and use the example of unexpectedly meeting a future romantic partner at, say, a bookstore. However, the actions of both parties in going to the bookstore are caused, the result of their own choices. But they did not know that they would meet a special person there. Meeting "by chance" in this context means they did not plan or predict the meeting. Their meeting was coincidental (i.e., lucky). They might have secretly hoped for such a meeting but did not know it would happen. The same applies to a "random number," a concept used by statisticians. A random number is a number taken from, for example, a "random number table," that you did not choose or expect, even though the table was created by a computer programmed in a certain way.

Now consider how people come to grasp the concept of causality experientially, starting with a newborn infant. Let me start by describing the daily life of a real newborn across the first twelve months. We will call this child Pat (P for short). In this period, P is pre-verbal and not yet able to walk unaided.

Here are some selected observations, partly chronological but with a lot of overlap:

- P reaches their hand out to try to touch a mobile; this goes on for weeks until P is able to grasp it.

- P pulls it; if it is attached to a mechanism that makes sound, he pulls it again.

- P pushes a ball away.

- P repeatedly tries to turn over when laid down; after weeks of trying P succeeds.

- When placed in a harness attached to a stand, P bounces up and down.

- P starts crawling everywhere and goes after the cat (who runs away).

- When P is ready to start eating solid food, P learns to grab food from the tray.

- As his skill develops, P throws food on the floor. As P gets older and learns that this is not particularly appreciated, P pushes food down into the high chair between his legs.

- P gradually learns to manipulate plastic boxes, fitting them clumsily (but not very consistently) into one another and taking them apart.

- While being bathed, P grabs toys and splashes them into the water.

- P crawls to the sofa and is lifted onto it, then tries to get down.

- When taken to the children's section of the local library, P goes after someone's iPad and tries to take library books off the shelves.

- P lifts himself up by the handle of a small, wheeled cart and pushes it across the room until it crashes into a wall; when the cart is turned around, P pushes it to the other end of the room until it crashes again.

- At about a year old, P becomes fascinated by containers and lids, first just getting the lid on and off. Then, it becomes about what can fit in different type of containers. When a stuffed lion won't fit into one of them, P gets frustrated and throws them both.

- When P does not want to take a nap, he throws all of his stuffed animals out of the crib and onto the floor.

- P becomes fascinated by his mother's swim cap and goggles and signals her by handing them to her to put them on over and over again. The same goes for her hats.

Later, usually in the second year, P tries deliberately to get his mother and/or father to do things by the use of words and gestures.

What is going on here? *It is quite obvious that much of P's daily life consists of doing uncontrolled causal "experiments" through trial and error. P is trying to control his or her own body and objects in the environment most of the day, every day.* Of course, infants only grasp even simple connections gradually, through many repetitions. They will reach, temporarily, some mistaken, implicit "conclusions" along the way—e.g., that pulling the ribbon tied to the crib railing will move a mobile or that a larger box will fit into a smaller box. Due to perceptual feedback, such errors are eventually corrected.

All this, of course, is years prior to the infant's ability to understand causality at the conceptual level. The child's experience and understanding of causality is solely perceptual; but this is the required base for later, conceptual understanding (see Harriman 2010; for an explanation of how causal understanding is tied to perception and thereby the process of concept formation, an inductive process, and also how physics progressed through the method of induction).

Nevertheless, mistakes aside, the causal connections that children eventually make are real. Children really do learn to control their own movements and to affect the actions of objects in the real world. Objects are not moved by magical or random forces. For example, children learn that a certain sequence of movements (grasping the handle, getting up, pushing while walking) will move a little cart across the room and that other sequences (screaming, slapping the side of the cart, grabbing a book) will not. *The child does not see an entity called necessity.* Necessity is a concept based on observation and inference, not by observing an actual entity called necessity. What the child learns to grasp is the connection between the object's identity and how it acts.

How do children progress, then, from an infant's perceptual knowledge to a conceptual grasp of causality that we have as adults? Here are some of the steps:

- By differentiating between objects; they learn through the senses that entities differ from each other in their attributes, such as size, color, shape, hardness, weight, temperature, taste, sound.

- They gradually form concepts of objects based on perceived similarity.

- They observe that different objects have different capacities for action. If they push on a small wheeled cart, it moves; if they push on a wall it does not. If they try to lift a small toy, they can; if they tries to lift their mother they can't. They see that the cat moves itself, but a pillow does not. If they suck on their bottle, they get milk; if they suck on a toy block they do not.

- They learn to connect specific attributes and actions. Big, heavy things are harder to move than small, light things. Round things roll across the floor more easily than cubes. Hot things cause pain. Soft things feel better against the skin than hard things.

- A corollary of this is that they eventually learn, in any given case, what specific attributes are relevant to a given action or outcome and which are irrelevant. For example, color does not affect how a ball rolls but the floor surface does. Shape and size affect what object will fit into what receptacle but sound and color do not.

As children learn language they frequently begin to bombard their parents with "why" questions sometimes to the point of parental frustration. They want to know what makes things happen, e.g. why does it rain? Answers such as "water condenses in the clouds" may be followed by further questions until the parent cannot answer.

What an infant or young child gradually learns from parents and others and through experience is that reality is lawful; things have a nature, an identity, that affects what they can do. The child learns to anticipate (predict) what will affect what; they develop foresight and a sense of control.

Ideally, they come to view the world as a sane, orderly place (if they are not in a war zone or the victim of parental abuse). Of course, when it comes to people, the conclusion may be different and the outcome sometimes tragic. An irrational adult or culture can do terrible damage, not just physically, but by making the infant or child—who cannot put it into words—feel or conclude subconsciously that the world does not have a firm identity, that other people are crazy, unlawful, unpredictable, incomprehensible, irrational, and painful. They may even conclude that it is somehow their fault. On the other side of that coin, a caring rational adult will help the child understand the world (including other people) and prevent the child from feeling unearned confusion, guilt, or self-doubt. An ideal parent helps create a sane universe for their child.

Children eventually learn to act based on their implicit (and later explicit) causal knowledge through conscious intent with an end in mind. The time scale is very short range at first, but with age children learn to direct actions past the range of the moment—they gradually engage in longer term, consciously goal-directed action. They learn to formulate and utilize plans as a means to their goal. They learn to use words, symbols that stand for concepts, and to use them to identify causal connections. As they get older, understanding causality, of course, gets more complicated. There are more objects, more attributes, more people, more locations, more delay between action and result, and chains of causation. Children have to learn to think. Their understanding of causality goes far beyond the perceptual level (though perception is always at the base) to the conceptual.

Some aspects of this: children have to learn to abstract out factors which may be correlates of causal connections but are not causal. They have to learn that causes are often combinations of factors. They (ideally) need to learn to introspect to identify what motivates their own actions. They have to try to understand other people and figure out who to trust, intellectually and morally. They need to learn to consider long range and not just short range consequences of their and others' actions. They need to become a rational adult through thought. Not everyone does this (see Chapter Eight).

Of course, determinists take issue here. Their argument, based partly on Hume, goes like this: it is true that a conscious goal or intent may precede action in space and/or time, so people naturally conclude that the intent caused the action. But this assumption, they say, is an illusion—just more folk psychology. For the determinist all life is like a magic show; what you experience as a causal agent is not real. You are simply being fooled. Intentional actions, they argue, are caused by the brain; the intent is an epiphenomenon (Wegner 2002).

The determinists' claim entails massive context dropping. What are they missing? Intentions (past the level of infancy) exist in a wider context than just a single, momentary desire or fantasy. Life requires logical sequences of consciously directed actions. Consider an adult going to buy groceries. The shopper has to be conscious. They have to know what groceries are and where they are sold. They have to choose a particular store. They may want to first gather discount coupons. They have to know what things they can buy there and how to get there (car, walking, bus) and/or what route to take. They have to have some idea of what they want and why they want it (e.g., to feed the family dinner). They have to have some idea of cost unless they are a millionaire. They have to take money or a credit card. They have to decide what day to go and what time of day to go. They have to have a written or mental list of items to buy, though that may be modified in the store. A mentally active shopper will look for special displays and daily discounts as well as foods that are health promoting (we hope) and value-priced, in addition to being tasty. Thoughts and actions have to be integrated and occur in a specific order; it will not work to shop mindlessly, then go home and make a grocery list for that day. Planning a route to the store will not help after arriving home. They cannot pay after they leave the store. *The logic of the order of intentions matters, because this determines the order of action.* Shopping may not be super complicated, but like most everyday activities it requires an orchestration of knowledge and actions.

Of course, the shopper must rely on their subconscious but not everything in it. They have to give orders that say, in effect: feed me the information I need to go shopping. A comatose shopper will never get to the store at all. If they are conscious but passive, or if the subconscious is not regulated by a purpose, they might end up at the zoo, a bar, the ballpark, or in front of the TV—based on non-purposeful associations based on one or more of their many brain modules and unchosen environmental stimuli. Such actions will still be caused, but they will not be logically related to a purpose. A passive shopper who somehow makes it to the store will tend to buy things they do not need and fail to buy things they do need.

Old-time behaviorists will claim that shopping trips are simply conditioned by past rewards and punishments—but people are not lab rats or house pets. Peoples' values determine what they will find rewarding or punishing, and they have the power to choose what to value and to choose their hierarchy of values. They also have the power to decide about time: what to pursue short range vs. what to plan and pursue long range. They have the power to acquire new knowledge and to make decisions about nutrition and prices. Every visit to the store will differ in specific ways from every other. A "conditioning" model, which is at root based on the assumption of mindless, subconscious determinism, is completely hopeless for understanding even something as basic as shopping—not to mention human action in general.

What about impulsive actions? Even impulsive actions have a cognitive context. Consider criminal actions; research by the world's leading expert on the criminal mind, Stanton Samenow, reveals that criminals think about committing crimes all the time (Samenow 2004). Criminal thinking is continuous and it is acted upon when they see that a promising opportunity has presented itself. Criminals have a form of moral code but it is a different code than that of law-abiding people; to them, the good is "what I want." It is not based on an abstract moral principle. This perverted value system underlies their crimes. Do they have the power to question it? Yes, but they may or may not choose to (see Chapter Eight).

Everyday action is based (consciously and subconsciously) on values and often relatively simple beliefs about causal connections and for everyday action, these often suffice. Most people get home in one piece and accomplish some chosen goals. However, not all causal connections are readily perceived. Diet is a good example. The connection between eating a specific food or certain types of foods and health is a complex issue for several reasons. First, the effects of diet are longer range than one's day to day activities. Second, it is not just one food but combinations of foods (nutrients) that determine health. Third, there are genetic factors that play into how specific foods affect you, for better or worse. Fourth, non-food factors (e.g., smoking, alcohol, exercise) affect health, too.

The principle here is that many outcomes are the consequence of multiple factors acting in concert or in some specific sequence and over time. Often people can figure out causal connections through thinking, based on previously acquired knowledge (e.g., reading health reports online or in print media). Of course, sometimes they cannot—or do not choose to try to figure things out.

Scientific studies are often required to sort out complexity. Understanding the human body has been one of the most challenging tasks in human history, and despite enormous progress, we are very far from being done. In science at least three major methods are used: mathematics, experiments (including with animals), and the minute (microscopic and sub-microscopic) identification of the parts of the body (e.g., cells, vessels, bacteria, viruses, and DNA). New technology is also vitally important.

Discovering cause and effect relationships here is incredibly difficult because there are so many parts to the body and they interact in very complex ways. This is far beyond the range of perceptual observation, though perception is always the starting point.

Mathematical analysis (small and big data) can suggest causal hypotheses. Formal experiments, in which key variables are controlled while the hypothesized causal fact is manipulated, can indicate the average effectiveness of drugs and surgical techniques (ideally with comparison or control groups). Even this is complicated because a drug can affect many bodily systems and work differently in different people. Examination of DNA and cells and their parts can give clues as to biological functions. New technology allows us to discover new entities and relationships and do it progressively faster.

Causality operates in the human body just like it does in the rest of the universe—the body does not operate at random—but understanding at this level requires enormous feats of abstraction. Science, if the mind is left free to think, progresses steadily with bursts of genius (e.g., Newton's Laws, evolution, the germ theory of disease), followed by endless incremental discoveries. Causal understanding starts with perception but must be supplemented by the acquisition of conceptual knowledge (Harriman 2010).

What about the human mind? We can observe what is in our conscious mind and what comes into awareness from the subconscious. We can formulate and identify goals and guide action towards them. How goal-directed action operates in living organisms is the subject of the next chapter.

# 4

# GOAL-DIRECTED ACTION

"Life is a process of self-sustaining and self-generated action" (Rand 1964; Peikoff 1991). Life is a goal-directed process. A goal is the object or aim of an action (Locke and Latham 1990).

A fundamental difference between living organisms and inanimate objects, a difference that makes goal-directed action necessary, is that life is conditional. In the case of inanimate matter, although entities can change their form (e.g., water can boil or freeze or turn to vapor; stars can collapse; rocks can be ground into dust), they face no fundamental alternative. Matter does not go out of existence when it changes its form. But if a living organism does not function to further its life, the life process goes out of existence. That is what death means. Physical matter remains but the living organism does not. To survive, living organisms need to take goal-directed actions which fulfill their needs. (I should note that I in no way subscribe to vitalism, the idea that some ineffable or mystical process controls life.) Goal-directedness is simply a description of the nature of the life process: goal directed action → goal attainment → life (or thriving).

The concept of goal-directed action has been the subject of much confusion. Part of the problem stems from the fact that there are actually, in humans, three different (though interrelated) types of goal-directed action. Furthermore, one of these types does not involve consciousness.

This has given superficial plausibility to a serious error: that goal-directed action applies to inanimate objects, such as machines.

To clarify these issues, we need to start with vegetative action.

## Unconsciously Goal-Directed Action

Living organisms are material entities, some of which possess the emergent property of consciousness. Every complex organism is composed of millions of cells of many different types that form an integrated whole. Their cells work though automatic chemical and electrical processes. Not counting single cell microorganisms (e.g., prokaryotes), plants are the most basic form of life. They have a structure that leads them to respond to external conditions in relation to their needs (e.g., turning their leaves toward the sun, sending roots into the soil to get water and minerals, repelling harmful fungi and bacteria, etc.), but this is not done consciously. Aristotle called this the vegetative level of life.

Animal and human internal systems are more complex than those of plants, but these systems are also partly vegetative; they operate automatically, without conscious direction. The heart, lungs, liver, kidneys, stomach, intestines, the senses, brain, nerves, blood vessels, immune system, and all the other body parts and systems work automatically, through specialization and intricate orchestration, to sustain the organism's well-being and survival. If the systems fail to work properly, the result is sickness or death.[17]

The unconscious, vegetative processes are teleological but, to repeat, they are not the result of any mysterious, non-material "élan vital" or supernatural directive. These goal-directed processes are the result of evolution. Any organism or species that did not have the needed unconscious goal-directed mechanisms simply did not survive and thus did not

---

17  Human beings, thanks to the faculty of reason and subsequent discoveries in medicine, can acquire some power to regulate how their body parts function based on conscious discoveries, but this is an add-on to what occurs automatically.

reproduce. (Aristotle did not know about evolution but he saw that organisms' parts had specific functions.)

Now consider a specific example of how vegetative, goal-directed action helps sustain life in human beings (Binswanger 1986, 4-5):

> ...my heart will be able to beat tomorrow only if I am alive tomorrow. But I will survive only if my blood is circulated today. The present blood circulation is thus an indirect cause of the future heartbeat. And since blood circulation is the *goal* of the heartbeat, this means that subsequent heartbeats are caused by the survival value of that action's goal, as attained in earlier instances of that very action....The vegetative [unconscious] actions of living organisms are teleological, i.e., goal-directed— because these actions have been naturally selected for their efficacy in attaining ends having survival value for the agent...in vegetative action, a *past instance* of the "final cause" functions as the efficient cause.

The same principle applies to other bodily systems. These systems, of course, all work in synchrony.

It should now be clear why analogies that equate the life process with cybernetic activity like that of a thermostat are fundamentally misguided. The goal of a thermostat qua thermostat is not to preserve itself or the heat pump or the house or even to manage the temperature. The thermostat has no goal of its own at all. Its existence is unrelated to what the household temperature is set at. To the extent that there is a goal involved, it is solely the conscious goal of the human builder and/or user, not of the machine. In contrast, homeostasis, the maintenance of a certain bodily stability such as temperature, promotes and is essential to life. The fact that inanimate objects can be moved or changed or exist in alternate states (depending on their nature and the causal factors impinging on them), does not make them goal-directed entities. The cybernetic analogy misses the essential point of what it means to be living—i.e., to act to promote survival and well-being.

The issue can be confused even by writers who otherwise do see living and non-living entities as different. For example, T. W. Deacon writes, "…both the molecular regulator of the cell and the engineered thermostat embody constraints that are *useful to some superordinate system*" (Deacon 2012, 396). But what is the system in the case of inanimate objects? Deacon acknowledges that the thermostat is regulated by human desires but still maintains that biological and engineering systems follow the same "pattern of behavior." But a behavioral approach is far too superficial. The critical issue is: what is behind the behavior? What does it accomplish? What is the superordinate system? In fact, there is no superordinate system in the case of the thermostat other than its human goal. The thermostatic system, the parts and their connections, are not integrated around the goal of preserving the thermostat (or heat pump), but rather that of making people comfortable.

An even more obvious example of the difference between machines and humans is another widely used example of a cybernetic machine: the torpedo. The goal of a torpedo, again set by its builders and users, is to destroy an enemy vessel by blowing itself up at the right time and place. *It is designed for self-destruction.* The only superordinate system which it serves is a human goal—that of self-preservation.

Cybernetics is a legitimate field of study, but engineering inanimate matter to serve human ends through feedback loops does not make the product a biological or goal-directed entity. No one can deny that living organisms are physically machine-like, but there is still a fundamental difference even at the physical level. *A living organism is a teleological "machine" in which every part and function serves, in an integrated fashion, to sustain itself* (Binswanger 1990). In the higher organisms, consciousness plays a critical role as well. The goal of life is life. Man-made machines only serve human ends.

## Perceptually Guided Goal-Directed Action

As noted, vegetative action functions solely at the non-conscious level. Although plants do not have exactly the same internal structure as the vegetative systems of animals, both have large amounts of DNA in common. But the lower animals represent a higher level of complexity, physiologically and cognitively, than plants. Although animals possess all the non-conscious or vegetative mechanisms noted in the previous section (internal organs, etc.) and many more, these are not sufficient to insure their survival. Animals have to move through their environment to identify food sources and avoid predators. Based on perceived similarities and differences they can make perceptual groupings (e.g., lions vs. antelopes) which in humans are the precursor to concept formation (Chapter Two). They have to find what they need to enhance and protect themselves. The evolution of consciousness in the form of sense perception makes such life-enhancing action possible. It is true that the processes underlying sense perception are unconscious, but the result is conscious.

What exactly does a perceptual consciousness make possible for animals?

1. Awareness of the world by means of the senses, especially sight, smell, touch, and hearing. Animals need to make perceptual discriminations, such as between friend and foe, nourishment and poison, safe and unsafe places and the like, and they need to know where they are in relation to other entities. They need to see objects and the motions of objects.

2. Desire, wanting things driven by their needs. Pursuing goals is not, as cyberneticists typically view it, simply to "remove discrepancies" between a goal and actuality. That could be achieved by eliminating goals. The goal is to actually get the valued object, such as food, because life depends on it. Discrepancy reduction is a correlate, not the motive of action. Animals want things; inanimate objects

do not. Wanting involves not just awareness of objects but emotion. Emotions contain action impulses to retain, protect, comfort, escape, or destroy other entities (Locke 2009).

3. Perceptual learning. This includes remembering places where they got food and water, where predators lurk, where mates hang out, and what and how to attack or to escape.

4. The regulation of action. The mechanics of movement itself (e.g., walking or running) are unconscious, set in motion by desires or goals, but the movement has to be consciously directed. The animal has to know where it is going and what it wants.

Aristotle called this the sensory level of life.

Even though animals cannot enhance their senses with instruments, or choose their own goals, or form concepts (see Chapter Two), consciousness is nevertheless critical to their survival. It is not just that they need a brain; they need to be aware and motivated in order to guide effective action. Animals whose consciousness was absent or not functioning (e.g., being in a coma due to brain damage) simply could not survive. Consciousness for animals is a critical link in a causal chain leading to life-preserving action.

## Conceptually Guided Goal-Directed Action

Man shares with the lower animals the basic internal structure of the body (the vegetative level) and the perceptual level of awareness, but this is not sufficient for human survival. Animals, on the average, have more acute senses and are faster and/or stronger than people and can eat and drink things that people could not tolerate. The capacity for conceptual thought (reason), despite the bafflement (and even hostility) of many scientists, has very obvious survival value, as illustrated in Chapter Two.

1. Using reason, we can, and need to, go beyond the perceptual level through the formation and use of concepts, magnifying man's cognitive capacity to an incalculable degree

2. We can create, by choosing our values, our own desires.

3. We can not only store (retain) perceptual memories, but also conceptual information, both inside the body (brain) and without (e.g., through the writing of books and computer or cloud storage). We are getting to the point that much of the world's accumulated knowledge can be accessed online.

4. We can think and plan long range, beyond the present and the immediate past and future.

Aristotle calls this the intellectual level of life, which includes conscious deliberation and foresight (Bandura 1997), both aspects of the conceptual level. This sets people, despite possessing the vegetative and sensory levels, apart from animals, just as the sensory level sets animals apart from plants. Through reason people can not only adapt to varied environments, but they can adapt environments, including changing environments, to their own needs though farming, irrigation, building, manufacturing, etc. Millions of species have become extinct in the history of the planet; a major reason, over and above the growth of human population, was that, without the faculty of reason, they did not have the capacity to adapt to change, especially climate change. Plant-eating dinosaurs needed to consume, in some cases, thousands of pounds of vegetation a day; when the climate changed it is presumed that they starved. They were unable to grow their own food. (True, they did not have hands, but hands would not have done them any good without the capacity to reason.) As noted, humans can even consciously intervene at the vegetative level by taking steps to prevent, relieve, or cure physical ailments.

Consider one more fact: chimps, who are repeatedly lauded for being just like us (due to 95% or more overlap in DNA), may face extinction despite having been around for at least six million years. Presumably this is because there are many people encroaching on their natural habitats and because they have no means of protecting themselves. In contrast, in only about 100,000 years the human (*Homo sapiens*) population has increased from maybe thousands to over seven billion (most of it in the last 2,000 years—and this is despite disease, natural disasters, starvation, numerous wars—and the population, like it or not, is still growing. Why this difference between species?

To repeat, we possess the faculty of reason and chimps do not. Considering the millions of discoveries made by humans which fostered the development of civilization, questioning the survival value of the rational faculty is beyond honest debate, as I explained in Chapter Two.

The rational faculty gives us the power, if we choose it, to take steps to help chimps survive (e.g., by building natural habitats), but they cannot lift a finger to help us. It also allows us to take steps to help both sick humans and sick animals survive in ways which are completely unknowable to animals (e.g., the whole field of medicine).

I noted in Chapter Two that the conceptual level, i.e., reasoning, can be wrong. Obviously there have been many disasters and tragedies caused by wrong ideas (goals and values) in human history (Peikoff 1982), but there have been enough men of reason (thanks especially to Aristotle, Newton, Darwin, Locke, and many others) to move civilization forward.

Human beings cannot survive by passively going on automatic and letting sense perception and their internal organs do all the work needed for survival. They must choose to pursue goals and discover the means to attain them in order to flourish. This includes thinking long range (across days, weeks, months and years), which is not possible to animals. It should be stressed that thinking long range does not violate the law of causality, with a future object causing action in the present. It is the *idea* of a desired future object or state, an idea held in conscious form (and stored, until the time for action arrives, in the subconscious), which regulates purposeful action (Bandura 1997; Seligman et al. 2013, 119-141).

Even defenders of consciousness may formulate purpose in strange ways. Deacon, for example, argues that purpose refers to "an essential absence" (Deacon 2012, 3). He means that the desired object is not yet attained, but in the most fundamental sense the concept of purpose is a presence; it's an idea in the mind, a real mental entity that guides action toward an outcome.

To summarize, goal-directed action separates the actions of living entities from inanimate matter. Life is conditional and must be furthered by action which fulfill the needs of the organism. In plants, action is automatic and unconscious. In animals, sense perception is added onto vegetative action. In humans, the rational faculty is added onto vegetative action and sense perception. Human survival and flourishing requires three types of integrated, goal-directed action. Humans can, for the most part, take the first two for granted since they are automatic. But reason requires deliberate self-regulation. (More on this in later chapters.)

# 5

# THE SELF

The concept of self, like that of goal-directed action, has been the object of a great deal of confusion. Some have claimed that the self is the peak of evolution. Others, especially determinists, argue that the idea is illusory (Wegner 2002, 342), a convenient fiction, which somehow humans need—a necessary illusion. Religionists often believe that man has an immortal soul or self that lives on in some form after biological death. Still others have ascribed selfhood not just to humans but also to single celled organisms (e.g., bacteria), and have claimed that humans are composed of numerous, nested selves—including a neural self (Deacon 2012). Animal psychologists argue that certain apes have the concept of self because they can recognize themselves in the mirror.

To bring order out of chaos, we need to start with this question: what fact of reality gives rise to the concept of self? *The starting point is our experience of being conscious.* "In every state of consciousness that you experience, part of it is the fact of the person who experiences. And in that sense you are implicit in every state of your consciousness" (Rand 1990, 255).

But how does the idea of a self become explicit? By introspection you can become conscious of being conscious. Introspection requires a conceptual faculty which includes the capacity to volitionally turn one's focus from external to internal. But the I or self is wider than just knowing that one is aware. *Each of us experiences ourselves as an entity, as a separate, integrated whole—something which thinks, feels, and acts a unit. The total self encompasses all of our attributes. These attributes include not only all aspects of one's consciousness including memories, knowledge, skills, values, perceptions, thoughts, and cognitive processes but also one's physical body, including all of its parts.*

It is important to add that *the self includes, by association, all of one's actions,* viz., I am someone who did this. There have been psychologists who have argued, "Well, your actions may be bad but that does not make you a bad person." But this depends on the type of actions and the total pattern of actions. A career criminal is a bad person. You are responsible for your actions. The same principle holds for good actions making you a good person.

The person who commits a crime cannot claim, "Well, it was my body that did it, not the real me, not my beliefs or my feelings." Human action is not disembodied. Though your self is the sum of your attributes, it is not experienced as a series of unconnected parts. The body does not go to Seattle while the mind goes to New York. (I am excluding fantasy here.) To repeat, the self is a unit. (There is no rational basis for positing a disembodied soul, i.e., a mind, in the absence of a body, including a brain, as noted in Chapter Two.)

We discover the different attributes and parts of ourselves through observation and abstraction, by selective focus. "Hey, look; there's my foot." We learn to identify and name various body parts and their functions. We can look at ourselves in the mirror.[18] We discover through introspection the various functions our minds can perform and its contents (e.g., perception, concept formation, learning, imagining, planning, thinking, evaluating, feeling, remembering, etc.). Still, we experience our attributes as

18   See Johnson's *How We Got to Now 2014* for a discussion of how the invention of the mirror not only helped Renaissance painters understand linear perspective, but also allowed people to see their own faces—which may have contributed to peoples' sense of individuality.

aspects of our whole selves; viz., this is my leg, my hand, my thought, my memory, my emotion, etc.

We have another, more indirect, source of information about ourselves: feedback from others. This does not mean that others always perceive us correctly (objectively). But if others respond to attributes we possess and value in ourselves, it gives us visibility—which means: a perspective on ourselves (e.g., our virtues) that we cannot easily get from the inside. (This insight comes originally from Aristotle, who said a friend was another self.)[19] Visibility does not mean approval as such but rather enhanced awareness. Others, of course, can give us negative or zero visibility through their reactions or non-reactions to attributes they find undesirable.

The concept of a self is neither fictional nor illusory. What would it mean to deny the self? (I am talking here metaphysically, not morally). It would mean denial of our body, which can be perceived directly or through a mirror. It would mean the denial of our consciousness, which is self-evident. It would mean denying that we exist as a unit, which is implicit in everything we do.

What determinists seem to object to at the deepest level, however, is not our experience of selfhood per se (though some see it as an illusion or a necessary illusion) but the premise that the self is an agent—that in some respect we are self-guided, that consciousness is efficacious. We have seen in previous chapters that consciousness is essential to human life, that it is fully consistent with causality, and that it guides action toward goals. Gradually we are peeling the determinist illusions away (see Chapter Seven for the full refutation). I will talk about free will at length in Chapter Eight.

---

19   See Locke and Kenner's *The Selfish Path to Romance* 2011 for a discussion of how showing your partner psychological visibility is an important contributor to romantic happiness.

## Self and Emotions

Contrary to popular belief, different attributes of the self are not, by their nature, at war with one another. The most common form of what is called the mind-body dichotomy (which stems from Plato and others, e.g., Freud) is reason vs. emotion. Many believe that a conflict between reason and emotion is built into human beings. But this is not the case. Let's start with what emotions are. Emotions (hormone imbalances and brain damage aside) are the form in which we experience subconscious value judgments (Locke 2009). Consider this example. If you meet a man waving a gun on the street nearby, your subconscious normally processes this as a threat to your life and well-being, and the automatic emotion you experience is fear. What causes this? First, your perception of the man waving the gun. You have stored knowledge about the nature of guns, bullets, their capacity for harm, your own mortality, the significance of your own location in relation to the gun, and how the gun is pointed, etc. This stored knowledge comes to mind automatically. Second, once you consciously perceive the situation, the subconscious makes a lightning fast value appraisal: this situation is a possible threat to your life. Fear is the form in which you consciously experience the appraisal of physical threat. Every emotion is based on a specific type of appraisal (Locke 2009). The fact that the amygdala, a primitive part of the brain, is involved in emotion does not refute the claim that stored ideas are involved. The brain is widely interconnected, as noted in Chapter One.

It is easy to validate this appraisal analysis with a mental experiment. If you did not see the man or the gun, or didn't know anything about guns, or were inside an armored truck, or did not care whether you lived or died, your appraisal would be entirely different. If there were no perceived threat, or you did not value your life, then you would not experience fear.

Now consider conflicting emotions. For example, you may feel conscious pride at something you accomplished because you know it was your own doing and was in some way important to you, but your subconscious may have filed a premise to the effect that pride is sinful. You therefore experience: "I feel pride, but I also feel guilt." The conflict is not at root between reason and emotion, but between two contradictory ideas: pride is good vs. pride is bad. The conflict is caused by the ideas you hold whether conscious or subconscious.

Psychological conflicts may be between one or more primarily conscious ideas and one or more ideas stored in your subconscious which you may not even be aware of. For example, you think making money is good but your subconscious may have filed and forgotten the idea taught in childhood Sunday school that love of money is the root of all evil; thus you experience feelings of both pride and guilt when you make money. Such conflicts are often resolvable by identifying the causes via introspection and then working to change one's ideas (Locke 2009). (It must be acknowledged that it is not always easy or even possible to change automatized emotions in severe cases such as early childhood abuse or PTSD, given our current knowledge. A solution will require advances in neuroscience, medicine, psychology and technology.)

Even when people have conflicts, they are conflicts within one person. Having multiple attributes and even contradictory goals and values does not create multiple selves in a normal person. All your beliefs, goals, and values are part of you. If you were one of those very rare people who actually experiences multiple selves (i.e., multiple personality disorder), it would be a sign of mental illness and would threaten your ability to function successfully. Even so, the selves are still yours. Your self includes your emotions and all the factors that cause them.

## The Essential (Core) Self

Although the concept of the self encompasses all of a person's characteristics, not all of them carry equal weight in regulating one's life. The mind matters more than one's big toe. To quote Ayn Rand, "A man's self is his mind—the faculty that perceives reality, forms judgments, chooses values" (cited in Binswanger 1986, 441). By implication this includes actions, which includes speaking out to defend one's values when the context is relevant, because values that are never acted on are just word sounds and thus not real values. If there is a contradiction between word and deed, the person lacks integrity. Actions, in the total context of your life, represent the more fundamental you (the conscious and subconscious combined), because they reflect what aspects of yourself are real—that is, taken seriously enough to be put into action. A person who professes honesty but lies is a liar. A person who claims to value justice but acts unjustly is unjust. A person who claims to value independence but conforms to every social convention without thought is a second-hander, a self of mirrors (and, in this case, an actual "social product," but by their explicit or implicit consent).

One can legitimately use the term soul to refer to one's mind and basic character and values, but I deny that there can be any kind of disembodied soul that floats around space for eternity. There is no mind without a body and brain.

## The Self and Change

It is obvious that everyone changes in some respects throughout life, e.g., through acquiring new experiences, knowledge, values, and skills—not to mention physical changes such as cell degeneration, replacement, and the entire process of aging. Every able-bodied person is continually taking new actions. But every human attribute does not change to something entirely different. You are still you. You are stuck with your heart and other organs for life unless you get a transplant (though age will make them less efficient). Your memory may weaken with age, but memories are still there. Your subconscious still retains information, barring brain damage. If you took an action, you cannot erase it; it is something you did. One's sense of self can evolve in various respects throughout the course of a lifetime; e.g., one can build one's character or lose it, increase one's knowledge or stagnate, pursue values or give them up, take care of one's body or abuse it. Criminals who want to be forgiven because "I am a different person now" are never a totally new entity and can't escape the fact that they did something wrong. A criminal who turns straight is: a criminal who turned straight. You are you, despite the changes, until you die. Even Alzheimer's victims up to a certain point retain remnants of their past selves.

## The Self and Society

Some social scientists resist viewing man as a separate, individual entity, arguing that the self, though separate in body, is, at root, a social product, a creation of society controlled by social norms or part of a higher level social organism. This claim presupposes the validity of environmental (social) determinism. (Is the theory of determinism forced on the determinists by social norms?) Although man does live in society (and would be hard put to survive without it) and thus learns from and trades with others, that does not make his individuality illusory. *Society as such is not an entity but an abstraction.* It refers to a group of individuals with at least some common values living and working together in the same area or country. It is not a "higher level" or mystical organism. It is not a mechanistic monolith composed of social automatons. It is not an omnipotent higher power. (The same holds for social institutions such as organizations.) Individuals' brains are not physically interconnected. Members deal with each other as individual members. Each person has the capacity to question what other members say and draw their own conclusions regarding the ideas that others offer.[20]

This should not be taken to imply that society is irrelevant to one's life. Among the most important gifts members of society can give each other, aside from mutual protection against enemies, are knowledge and

---

20  For a brilliant fictional but illuminating portrait of the soul of a conformist or second hander, see Ayn Rand's depiction of Peter Keating in *The Fountainhead* 1943.

trade. Through knowledge and economic trade, members create the values and wealth that make human survival and happiness possible. And, of course, within society one can find friendship and romantic love (Locke and Kenner 2011). By actively choosing one's friends and partners and by creating and changing situations, one can create one's own social situations.

## The Self and Matter

The concept of self has no meaning with respect to inanimate matter or to non-conscious organisms such as plants or bacteria—to entities with no mind (contrary to Deacon 2012, 466). A brick or a tree does have an *identity* (a nature) as do all entities (cf. the law of identity, noted in previous chapters), but their natures do not include consciousness. They cannot be self-aware because they are not aware at all. What would the term self refer to with respect to a bacterium or a banana? Nothing beyond the fact that they are something particular.

## Do Apes have a Self?

What about apes? Apes and other animals are, of course, conscious. This is not the same as being self-conscious. To the degree we can infer that apes have some form of a self, based on mirror studies, it has to be a very primitive, pre-conceptual form of it, consisting simply of perceptual self-recognition. (It is not clear that all apes have this capacity.) Apes would not be able to abstract out all the attributes of a self because that would require conceptual functioning. They do not possess the faculty of reason and cannot introspect. Reason is the peak (the most advanced stage so far) of cognitive evolution; the ability to have a concept of self is just one manifestation of the mind's capacity to form concepts. The second edition of the *Oxford Dictionary* has over 170,000 entries (i.e., concepts), although some of these are proper nouns. I have never seen an ape dictionary.

One might still ask, however, since apes are conscious: how do they experience themselves from the inside? This is a difficult question to answer; we would have to put ourselves inside the ape's mind and switch off our rational faculty. What would be left? Apes are conscious but cannot be conceptually self-conscious as described earlier. They have perceptions, desires, and memories, as noted in Chapter Four. But would they experience themselves, in some form, as single units even if they could not abstract out (identify) their many attributes? We will have to speculate here. Household pets can learn the names people give them and can learn through rewards to come hither or perform when signaled; so that may be as close to a unit as its gets for them. "Fido, come." "Hey, that's me," but they would not even be able to put that much into such a sentence or understand "that's" or "me." Nor would they understand the abstract meaning of "come."

A name (proper noun) is not a concept, but a concrete word sound associated through repetition to a concrete entity or action. Whatever form of self an animal might have, it could not be anything remotely like the human concept of self.[21]

It appears that not all animals (e.g., cats) recognize themselves in the mirror. If ape species are unique in this respect, one has to assume that their brain structure is different in some way from that of other animal species. But that does little to close the chasm between apes and us.

---

21  I have long wondered about the desperation of animal psychologists to show that the lower animals, especially chimpanzees, are very much like us. At first I wondered if it was an attempt to support the theory of evolution, but the theory does not require evidence based on animal experiments; DNA evidence and ancient human fossils are quite sufficient. A second possibility is that the researchers want and can get research funding by pretending that animals can throw light on human cognitive abilities. A third possibility, revealed in various comments in the press and elsewhere, is that they want to denigrate humans by showing that we are not as superior as we think we are. I am still waiting for chimps to build labs, do experiments on us, and write books about those experiments.

## Self-Related Concepts

This chapter is not a treatise on theories of the self, but I will mention a few related, narrower concepts. There are over eighty "self" words in the *Oxford Dictionary*. (A few refer to mechanisms such as self-winding watches, but this does not mean that a watch has a self.) A human example is: the *self-concept*. This refers to what kind of person one sees oneself to be. Usually this does not refer to one's whole person, but to selected attributes—e.g., I am an intelligent, hardworking, friendly, honest, somewhat attractive 26-year-old female student. The *subjective self* (the self one believes one has or wants to have) may or may not correspond to the objective self, the individual's actual attributes. (A dishonest person may see themselves as honest; a smart person may see themselves as dumb.) Strominger, Knode and Newman 2017 note that people have what they call a "true self" which is centered around a belief in their own moral virtue. However, the true self may not, in fact, be true (which the above authors acknowledge). The psychological consequences of discrepancies between the subjective and objective selves is beyond the scope of this book—but it is not beneficial to be at war with reality.

The concept of *self-esteem* refers to the individual's overall judgment of his own efficacy to deal with life exigencies and one's judgment of one's moral worth. (Locke, 2006-7). High self-esteem is an appraisal that one can handle life's challenges (direct one's life successfully) and is a good person according to some value standard. A self-report of self-esteem, like that of the self-concept, may not be accurate., may not be the true self. Through various defense mechanisms, self-esteem may be faked—up to a point. Pseudo self-esteem, however, is quite fragile because it is divorced from reality or based on irrational standards (Samenow 2004). Genuine self-esteem is positively associated with happiness and negatively associated with anxiety, self-doubt, and depression (Orth and Robins 2014, 381-387).[22]

---

22   A discussion of theories regarding the cause of self-esteem are beyond the scope of this book, but see Locke, 2006-7 for a detailed discussion.

*Self-efficacy* refers to a person's judgment as to how well they can perform specific types of actions (Bandura 1997). Whereas self-esteem is general, self-efficacy is task- or domain-specific (e.g., getting good grades, playing basketball, investing money, getting dates). Further, self-esteem is evaluative, whereas self-efficacy, as such, is descriptive (though it may have evaluative connotations). Self-efficacy is affected by past performance and one's assessment of the meaning of past performance (was it luck or skill?). It also has a causal effect on future performance as well as goals, commitment, and response to feedback.

# 6

# THE LIBET STUDIES: MUCH ADO ABOUT ALMOST NOTHING

Laboratory experiments conducted by Libet and others (Libet 1985; Bode et al. 2011; Bode et al. 2014) are cited repeatedly by determinists as strong evidence for the theory of determinism. Though there have been some trenchant critiques of the studies (Bandura 2008; Mele 2011), there is more to be said. Actually, the experiments do not prove determinism at all and are, in my opinion, poorly designed, misinterpreted, and preposterously overgeneralized. I will identify the flaws and demonstrate why looking at the studies more closely leads to very different conclusions than those reached by Libet and his supporters.

## Libet

Libet's typical study, referenced above, went like this: subjects were brought to a lab and hooked up with sensors on the scalp to record brain activity and on the wrist to record wrist movements. They were told to flex their wrists whenever they wanted to (no time limit) and to indicate when they first felt the urge to flex (wanting to move) using a timer (indicating the position of a spot of light on an oscilloscope or a moving clock hand). They did this forty times. Subjects were told not to plan their movements (though some did) but to act "spontaneously." It was found that a readiness potential (RP) in the brain—an electrical signal that some believe normally precedes voluntary action—occurred, on average, about 550 ms before the wrist movement. The so called "intent" to act was typically reported about 200 ms before wrist movement. In other words, the RP or brain activity preceded the reported intent by 350 ms (Libet 1985). In sum, the sequence was: RP, Reported Intent, Movement.

The conclusion many have drawn from the "spontaneous" part of the study and others like it is that the brain, rather than the mind (consciousness), ultimately regulates action and that conscious "intent' is an epiphenomenon, though Libet's position on the latter is not fully clear. Libet argues from additional experimental evidence that people can volitionally veto the wrist movement by changing their minds, so that there is free will not to act (to inhibit action), even if there is no free will to act. This is bizarre, because choosing not to do something is still a choice; if a person chooses not to do A, that means they are choosing B instead (e.g., rather than flexing my wrist, I will keep my wrist steady and keep daydreaming). Libet admits, further, that vetoing itself might be initiated by the brain, so even his qualification remains in doubt.

## The Flaws

Let's now look at flaws in the study.

1. The fundamental flaw is *overlooked purpose.*  Libet and his followers claim that "intent" is not the prime mover of action. But their own experiment shows otherwise. All subjects were assigned a goal before the experiment started, i.e., to respond on impulse at some chosen point. What would have resulted if they had been invited to the lab and allowed to just sit there (while the experimenter was supposedly doing something with the equipment or pretending to handle an emergency)? Presumably the subjects would have done nothing other than daydream. *The entire experimental setup requires the subjects to have a goal—a purpose.* (As noted, subjects actually

had about forty trials, so forty deliberate wrist flexes were required as expressions of the initial goal.) Thus the only issue left is timing: *when* will the goal be realized during each trial? So the setup was this: *an assigned conscious goal to be implemented allegedly at whim.* By focusing mainly on whims, Libet and fellow determinists have dropped the full context of the study, not to mention the full (and much wider) context of human action. But there is more.

Libet indicates very briefly in his report that in another experiment they told some subjects to flex their wrist at a preannounced time, presumably set by the experimenter, and that this led to the longer, more intense and prolonged RPs. Why would this be? Presumably because subjects took more time to anticipate and plan. But Libet totally fails to acknowledge the further implications of this alternative design. *It means that the subjects had a specific goal or purpose (respond at time X) rather than a general goal (respond at some time) and that this preceded and logically had to cause the RP. The only difference between this and the main experiment was in the latter the specific goal (time) was chosen later though the choice was required by the general goal.*

This means that the two types of study were not fundamentally different. Both responses are caused by purpose but in the study with the more general purpose subjects chose the time of implementation.

As noted, without the initial goals we can assume there would be no RP, no intention, and no action at all. In the popularized study, if there is a subconscious cause of the initiation of the short RP that does not depend on the initial conscious goal, Libet does not tell us what it is or how it could even arise. Claiming that the brain "decides" is a claim, not an explanation (see point # 5 below).

Subsequent studies by others using different tasks and brain measurements have replicated Libet's results and with even longer time intervals (e.g., ten minutes), even between brain signals and intent plus action (Soon et al. 2008, 543-45). This implies that the actions, which require only a fraction of a second to execute, were not spontaneous at all, despite the instructions. The human mind does not go inert just because you are instructed to act without planning. The mind is always active. To see what was going on, as noted above, you would need continuous reports of the subjects' cognitive processes.

These researchers are not aware that there is a whole field of literature in which subjects set a goal to take some action in the future and at the same time formulate a conscious implementation plan (e.g., when situation X arises I will do Y). The studies show that the goal can be executed weeks or months later when the relevant situation is perceived. The goal does not have to be consciously recalled later; obviously the goal is stored in the subconscious (Oettingen, Wittchen, and Gollwitzer 2013). This research program is a good example of recognizing the interaction of the conscious and subconscious in everyday life.

Further, there are over 1,000 scientific studies showing that conscious goals affect action, not to mention what we know from our daily experiences (Locke and Latham 1990 and 2013). The lag time between goals and action in these experimental studies has ranged from one minute to twenty-five years (Locke and Latham 2013).[23] Given this, are microseconds of any great significance?

Given what we know, it is not valid to generalize from Libet's results to a theory of determinism. Add to this the fact that the task was so simple that the human mode of functioning (reasoning, including long range thinking) was virtually ruled out—or at least officially prohibited.

What is overlooked at root in the Libet and Libet-like studies is the fact that human action is characteristically goal-directed, as noted in Chapter Four. This is not to deny that we can be mentally passive and let the subconscious take over at times, but this is not a template for successful thriving.

There are other problems with the Libet-type studies.

---

23   See also Sprang and Levine 2013.

2. *The lack of introspective reports.* Libet had the subjects introspect, but only superficially. We can assume that the subjects were mentally active or at least alert during the entire interval before acting. But we have no idea what was going through the subjects' minds throughout. They were told not to plan but some did. But even those who did not, and were trying to act spontaneously, must have been thinking of something. To know the full picture, the subjects should have been thinking out loud the whole time so their thoughts could be recorded. Subjects may have had urges or fleeting or changing plans they did not report, which would preclude having measurements of a series of possibly correlated RPs. Not all experiments need thinking out loud data, but it is relevant here because subjects could decide to act or not act whenever they wanted to. However, having subjects think out loud presents a problem in Libet-type studies. A neuroscientist acquaintance told me that if subjects were to think out loud, that would ruin the brain recordings due to some form of interference. Now, if true, this is very convenient for determinists, yet represents a serious problem that needs to be overcome. Further, it brings up a question: if thinking disturbs the reaction potentials, why does it? Are thoughts affecting brain activity, heaven forbid? If so, what does that imply? This whole issue is a Pandora's Box that needs to be opened.

3. *Intentions.* Subjects did not report (through wrist flexing) actual intentions at all, but rather "urges" or desires to act. These are not necessarily the same thing. An intention would be: "I am going to flex right now." An urge is "I feel like acting or want to act now," but feelings do not always lead to action. (Libet did say that subjects reported vetoing urges.) Would measuring actual intent lead to the same result as felt urges? We have no way of knowing. (I discussed the issue of intentions and their cognitive context in Chapter Four).

4. *Measurements.* There are potential measurement problems in the study. First, actually forming an intent takes a finite amount of time (and different times for different intentions—e.g., the intent to buy a house vs. the intent to follow a story on the internet vs. the intent to flick one's wrist). Even simple intentions may involve pondering, conflict (should I act now or wait?), and changing one's mind. Intentions are an ongoing process and may come and go before a final resolution is made. Libet assumes intentions occur in a finite instant but surely developing them has a duration. Second, putting an intent into words, which is not always done in everyday life, also takes a finite amount of time. The mind works faster than the mouth. (It's estimated that thinking in words is about three times faster than speaking in words.) Third, putting words into action takes a finite amount of time as well. Fourth, reading a cursor (sense perception) takes a finite amount of time, though Libet presents evidence that these last two may not be a problem (e.g., the intent to action time lag is about 200 ms, consistent with his data). I saw no evidence that Libet or others made any attempt to calculate the typical duration of the first two processes. Surely there must be a lag between beginning the process of forming an intent and everything that follows? I don't know of anyone who has tried to make such calculations. If some subjects engage in self-deliberation, it could throw off some of the assumptions Libet made about timing and intervals. The full sequence would most likely take longer than he assumes. Would more complete information of the types noted above affect the interpretation of the results? We have no way of knowing.

5. *Why do the RPs arise?* There is a certain mystery to the Libet results that no one has pointed out. If the RP is regulated by some subconscious event which is the real cause of action, and the "intent" is an epiphenomenon (or a link in a causal chain, which Libet at times

implies), then what causes the RP to come up in the first place and why does it arise at the exact time it does, rather than at some other time (intent aside)? What causes the RP in the Libet experiment to arise at all? And why does an intent follow it or even have to be involved? If it has to be involved, what exactly is its role? Does the RP arouse the intent by itself?

These issues need further exploration.

## Whim

We can ask one further question: although reason is man's main means of survival, do people in the real world ever act on subconscious whim (with no prior goal or plan), even if daily life is normally purposeful? The answer is obviously yes, as noted in Chapter Two. Acting on whim does not mean that the mind is blank except for a single whim. A person who is passive could experience a whole sequence of whims mixed with daydreams and non-purposeful associations.

Go back to my grocery shopping example in Chapter Three. One may consciously choose the day, the store, the time, the grocery list, and take corresponding actions. But then one may get to the checkout counter, spy a candy bar and grab it (RP or no RP), even though one had no intent to buy candy when planning the shopping trip. To repeat from Chapter Three, the subconscious can become "activated" in two obvious ways: (1) by automatically connecting to a chosen purpose (e.g., a shopping goal will automatically connect with a store location and route) and (2) by connecting to something external or a prior thought. When the conscious mind is passive at a given moment, there are, of course, degrees of purposeful focus (a subject I will address in Chapter Eight). Being purposefully goal-directed is a choice.

Even acting on whim, however, has a cognitive context; the impulse has to be tied to some subconscious value appraisal including ethical premises (e.g., the person could buy the candy, shoplift, or shoot the clerk and run). Everyone's impulses are not the same. Nor are the cognitive processes that precede it.

Of course, living one's whole life on whim is a recipe for disaster. A human being cannot survive without thought or long range planning. (A moocher or cognitively disabled person could survive only by the dint of the thinking and effort expended by others.) Someone who has brain damage at the site of their inhibition center is seriously disabled.

## Subconscious Priming

There is a large literature separate from the Libet studies that are cited with equal gusto by determinists who argue that priming proves that people's lives are run by the subconscious. These studies come mainly from within social psychology. Subconscious priming is a genuine phenomenon but there is no proven theory behind it (Locke 2015, 408-14).

Here is an example of a priming experiment: participants are asked to unscramble a set of words to make a meaningful sentence. In the primed group perhaps 60% of the sentences include an achievement-related word (e.g., excel, win, persist, try, etc.). A comparison group is given only neutral words like tree. Then both groups are given a simple task to perform, and the primed group performs better, even though these participants do not guess the purpose of the experiment. There is no validated theory to explain how priming works, but obviously something is being aroused by the prime words. This, of course, can also happen in everyday life. But it does not follow that our lives are controlled by subconscious associations. After all, we are deluged by hundreds (if not thousands) of stimuli in our everyday environment, but we do not go lurching mindlessly in one direction and then another.

This obvious fact has not stopped them, as is the case with the Libetians, from making grandiose claims about human action. Two eminent, priming champions' have claimed, that "...most of a person's everyday life is determined not by their conscious intentions and deliberate choices but by mental processes that are put into motion by features of the environment and that operate outside of conscious awareness and guidance" (Bargh and Chartrand 1999, 462). Claims like this are totally arbitrary. The claim is even false on its own terms. Priming is not done with comatose subjects. The people unscrambling sentences have to be aware of the words, some rules of sentence construction, and accepting of their assigned goal (to unscramble twenty sentences). They also have to find their way to the laboratory. Everyday life is a million times broader and more complex than priming tasks.

What would be a proper conclusion to reach about the Libet and priming studies? Not determinism. These studies are merely an illustration, if understood correctly, that human life and action involve the conscious and subconscious working together. This is fully in accord with our everyday experience. If we are deluded about this partnership, then wrist movement, impulse studies, and priming studies are not a valid means of disproving it. And if we are deluded about our beliefs, then aren't the Libetians and primers also deluded in claiming knowledge? After all, they would have to admit that their theories are themselves the result of subconscious (brain) impulses which control their lives, which includes their thoughts. Which means: they just couldn't help what they believe, though Libet might say that they can veto their beliefs. But, if so, how do they ever get to the truth?

This brings us to the next chapter, which exposes the fundamental contradiction of determinism.

# THE FATAL FLAW
# IN DETERMINISM

In the introduction I defined determinism as the doctrine that everything we think, do, feel, believe, decide, etc. is caused by factors outside our control—that we have no choice with respect to any aspect of our lives. Although there are various theories as to what determines us (e.g., instincts, supernatural entities, fate, or society), an increasingly popular view today comes from neuroscientists and their followers, who claim that we are controlled by our physical brains (including the subconscious) in conjunction with factors in the environment which trigger brain activity.

Nevertheless, all forms of determinism suffer from the same fatal flaw. The theory of determinism is incompatible with its own content. It commits the fallacy of self-exclusion (Peikoff 1991; Binswanger 2014).

Let's see why. If determinism claims you have no choice about your actions or thoughts or the views that you hold, then determinism applies to your belief in the doctrine of determinism. It means that you could not help believing it. The same would have to apply to those opposing determinism. There could be no way of deciding who is correct in such a dispute if all beliefs are imposed on people. Claiming that determinism is true while your theory claims that you are compelled to believe it (meaning that you are not free to judge truth or falsity at all) is a contradiction.

Although sense perception is a given and is automatic, conceptual knowledge is neither. It has to be validated. (Validation means demonstrating that something is true). One has to choose to function above the perceptual level and one can make errors. One can perceive a group of four rocks without effort or the need for any validation. Forming the concept of rock (and later mineral) and discovering mathematics (separating numbers from entities) requires reasoning. The acquisition (which means validation) of conceptual knowledge requires one to go through specific procedures in addition to in sense perception.

Let's say that a scientist wanted to determine whether alcohol consumption puts automobile drivers at risk for accidents. How would they go about it? They would need to:

- Understand concepts such as alcohol, driver, automobile, mathematics, objectivity, accident, risk, safety, causality, and many others.

- Gather data from previous studies relevant to the subject, e.g., accident records showing alcohol involvement based on tests of blood alcohol level; studies of drivers in controlled experiments driving on an obstacle course after consuming alcohol; laboratory studies showing the effects of alcohol on reaction time, risk assessment, and motor control; studies showing the effects of various doses of alcohol; studies involving representative samples of drivers (teenagers to seniors; males and females).

- Conduct and/or evaluate studies of how alcohol affects the brain and how the body metabolizes it.

- Examine all the evidence using mathematics, i.e., statistics (including deciding what measurements and tests to use).

- Decide whether there was a safe level of alcohol in the blood, which would require a specific definition of safe based on a reasonable standard of safety.

- Integrate all the data into a non-contradictory whole, including the evaluation of studies that seemed non-supportive of the predominance of the evidence.

Observe that this research process would require conceptual understanding, mental effort, and numerous choices or decisions. A good researcher would have to make the discovery of truth their fundamental mindset: this mindset requires looking at all the facts and working to reach objective conclusions (e.g., not letting emotions or bias cloud their judgment). But none of these choices would be possible if determinism were true. You would do what you were programmed to do and conclude what you were programmed to conclude.

Consider some examples of what could happen if the alcohol researcher could not make any choices; if everything they did was determined by factors outside their control. For example, they might be determined (caused) to:

- Have an unknown motive other than discovering the truth.

- Have a mistaken or impoverished or distorted grasp of the needed concepts (e.g., alcohol is a solid liquid; a driver is someone who sits in the back seat; an automobile is an electronic toy).

- Gather no information, irrelevant or wrong information, or incomplete (though available) information.

- Misinterpret or fudge the data, use biased sampling and statistics, do erroneous blood tests, study the wrong parts of the brain, take wrong measurements.

- Ignore contradictions, fail to integrate all of the data, include only results that conform to a bias or provide a positive emotional experience.

A determinist might argue: but there are procedures to prevent these mistakes. The problem is that a determinist cannot choose which procedure to follow. These would be regulated by uncontrollable causes. The determinist could not even know what procedures were actually needed or followed; that belief would be determined, too. Worse yet, the determinist would have no way of knowing what determined their actions because any such conclusion would also be determined.

Advocates of determinism cannot escape this fundamental contradiction. They want to claim knowledge, but this requires them to make the choices needed to gain knowledge—yet determinism asserts that they cannot make actual choices. *Determinists have to assume that they themselves are outside the deterministic nexus when reaching any conclusion; that they were free to make choices and reach conclusions based on their thinking rather than simply being pre-programmed.*

The determinist might claim: "I just looked at the evidence and by a process of reasoning concluded that determinism was true. The reasoning of the supporters of free will is just wrong." But determined beings cannot reason at all! Reasoning is a process of conceptual abstraction and integration, not a process of mechanical causation. A fully mechanical entity like a computer can be programmed to print words, but it cannot understand what it is doing. It cannot control or evaluate its programming. The validity of its printouts has no meaning except in relation to the uncoerced cognitive judgments of its human programmers. Qua computer, it is cognitively inert. Failing the Turing Test (being fooled by a computer programmed to "communicate" with you) doesn't prove anything except that you can be fooled, especially if you do not see the machine or have limited interaction. Whatever operations a machine performs, whatever its output, it has no choice. Everything is implanted.

Determinists repeatedly claim that free will is an illusion (Wegner 2002). But how would they be able to tell the difference between reality and illusion if they had no choice as to what to believe? Given their premise, determinism could just as well be an illusion as free will.

Pro-science determinists such as neuroscientists claim that human beings are machines, but this is only half true. Our physical bodies do obey the laws of physics and chemistry, though teleologically (Chapter Four), but that is not the whole story. Consciousness, though dependent on the brain, is not reducible to matter, as I noted in Chapter Two. The capacity to reason sets us apart from inanimate objects and also from the lower animals, which are conscious but can only function at the perceptual level.

*The fundamental problem, then, is this: determinism destroys the entire field of epistemology; the field which establishes the means and criteria for conceptual knowledge. This means it destroys the possibility of all conceptual knowledge, including philosophy and science—which includes neuroscience.*

One might ask: couldn't what a determinist says be true? That could only mean: couldn't some of the determinist's word sounds correspond to reality (e.g., 2+2=4)? Yes, but another determinist might claim that 2+2=5. How could they know who was right?

The contradiction of determinism has very rarely been acknowledged. One notable exception is Nobel Laureate and physicist Stephen Hawking, who recognizes the problem in his world famous best seller on the history of time (Hawking 1996). He tries to resolve the issue by invoking Darwin's theory of evolution. Hawking argues:

> "...some individuals are better able than others to draw the right conclusions about the world around them and then to act accordingly. These individuals will be more likely to survive and reproduce and so their pattern of behavior and thought will come to dominate." [People, he says, have] "reasoning abilities" (20-21).

This last is true, but there is a problem. We know from history that wrong ideas can exist for millennia (e.g., theories about the causes of disease, the existence of individual rights). Both free will advocates and determinists have survived. So natural selection could not tell us who was right in disputes. It is true that we possess the faculty of reason, but, again, reason does not give us automatic knowledge. Knowledge has to be discovered and validated by a certain process, as noted earlier. If one cannot regulate the process, there would be no way to discriminate between fact and fiction. Of course, people are far more likely to thrive if they possess and act on objective knowledge but first such knowledge has to be discovered and then accepted and then implemented. Over 200 years after the Declaration of Independence (and over 300 years since John Locke's Second Treatise of Government), most people in the world still live (and die) under dictatorships.

There is a bizarre irony in the theory of neuroscientific determinism. If we do not have the power to reason, to regulate our cognitive processes, then we are reduced to accepting what is implanted by some power higher than our rational minds—not a supreme being, according to neuro-determinists, but something like a supreme physical object: our brain. This brings determinism perilously close to a form of scientific mysticism: *epistemology would be replaced by the equivalent of materialistically caused revelation*—revelation because it would be beyond rational understanding. The irony is that determinism has been presented as the only view consistent with objective science, whereas it actually makes all science impossible.

To reiterate, it has been argued that we can know without knowing that we know, or proving that we know. It may be true that a determinist emits words sounds which are true to reality, but they could never know that they know.

Nor is it only science that determinism makes impossible. It also makes morality and moral judgment impossible.

## Determinism, Morality and Justice

Many have asked the question: if everyone is determined, then criminals could not help what they do, so wouldn't legal punishment be unjust? Given that premise, the answer is yes, of course. But determinists offer a defense, known as the consequentialist argument (Kane 2005).[24] It argues that the punishment of crimes that people could not help committing should still be used in order to deter other people from committing crimes. Punished criminals thus serve as exemplars, warning people not to break the law; thus, they argue, law and order is preserved and social anarchy is prevented. In this view, seeing other people get punished "conditions" those who have not yet broken the law. Punishments do not violate individual rights in this view, because rights presuppose freedom of choice—which determinism denies.

There are two serious flaws in consequentialism. First, it evades the contradiction of determinism. Consequentialism assumes that law enforcers can make fair, objective judgments. *But those who will mete out the punishments cannot be outside determinism. Their choices and actions would be determined just like those of the criminals.* Thus law enforcers would not be free to make fair, rational judgments about guilt or innocence with respect to the alleged criminal acts, nor rational judgments about what type of punishment to give for any given crime. Nor would they be able to make any objective conclusions about how well their punishments were working. They would only be able to think and act according to their own past conditioning. This would make the whole law enforcement process arbitrary and mindless, even given the narrow goal of deterrence—determined people punishing determined people. Biological robots controlling biological robots. This might make a bizarre science fiction movie, but it is hopeless as a model for a real society.

Second, to make matters worse, consequentialists often attempt to induce guilt among people who believe in real justice by obfuscating what justice really means. They imply that the desire for justice, which they call retribution (a term which can imply vigilantism) is immoral. They assert

---

24   Kane's work is based on Honderich, Pereboom and others-see Kane reference. Note: consequentialism comes in many varieties but this one is most directly relevant to the issue of legal punishment.

that punishment for crimes is cruel and based only on wanting alleged criminals to suffer; but this makes the desire for justice simply psychological. The fundamental issue, however, is moral; law abiding people want criminals to get their just deserts. They want to live in a moral society in which people who violate rights give up, in some suitable (proportionate) form, their own rights.[25] People want their own rights protected from those who would initiate physical force (or fraud) against them. Punishing people (whom the consequentialists claim cannot help what they do) for the purpose of political manipulation has frightening totalitarian implications. It is the consequentialists who should feel guilty for advocating views which would destroy the whole concept of a moral society. Their only defense would have to be: "Hey, we couldn't help it—we were conditioned to think this way!"

A psychological point needs to be made here: I do not believe that anyone can fully believe in determinism, even if they claim to. By that, I mean that they could not consistently act on it. They may give lip service to it, thinking they are being good scientists, or be influenced up to a point by determinist propaganda—but that does not mean that they accept it all the way down to the depths of the subconscious. If a person, in the midst of despair, somehow managed to fully accept determinism, they would be unable to function as a human being. The result would be some version of self-induced paralysis at best, or suicide or psychosis at worst. They would become the helpless robots that determinists claim we all are. There have been people who claim that they fully accept determinism and say they are quite happy about it. But how do they know determinism is true or even that they are happy? One can be confident that these people go through life making choices every day.

---

25  A point needs to be made about capital punishment. Though forfeiting one's life in return for first degree murder is just, there is another issue to consider. Human beings are fallible and thus people can be wrongly convicted; in the case of the death penalty, exonerating evidence sometimes comes too late. So a valid argument can be made in favor of life imprisonment.

Since the doctrine of determinism is self-refuting and thus divorced from reality, then free will in some form must exist. But showing that determinism is wrong does not constitute a theory of free will. Such a theory would have to specify just what free will consists of, and why that particular form of free will is valid as compared to other theories. It would also have to show the limits of free will: what it is and also what it is not. These issues are the subject of the next chapter.

# 8

# WHAT FREE WILL IS—AND IS NOT

## Failed Attempts to Defend Free Will

It is not the case that free will has no defenders; there have been many. But they have not been able to get the job done. I will discuss here the three most popular contemporary views that purport to support, or partly support, free will.

**Religion.** As noted in the Preface, there is disagreement within religion about free will. But since religion is based on faith and/or revelation, there is no way to validate either position within that framework. Thus I will not discuss religion further.

**Compatibilism.** Compatibilism is the view that determinism and free will are in some respect both true. Determinism says that in the same circumstance you could not have acted otherwise than you did. Free will says that you have the power of choice and could have acted differently under the same circumstances. Compatibilism argues that in some respect you are both determined and free. (This is similar to and is often seen as what is called "soft" determinism, as contrasted with "hard" determinism, which claims there is no room at all for personal choice.) I should note that compatibilist formulations are continually changing, and it would take a whole book to cover the different views and to keep up with the ever-evolving and often convoluted versions (Kane 2011). However, I will focus here on the two most common compatibilist arguments.

- Compatibilists argue that you are free to make choices, that is, to do what you want to do, to act on your feelings or desires, providing you are free from physical coercion. In this theory, however, you are not free to choose your desires. (One version says that you can have desires for desires but such a view readily becomes an infinite regress.) This means that in the last analysis, you are not in control. All causes of action in the end would have to be coercive—that is, irresistible, regardless of whether the causes are internal (brain, genes, desires) or external (environment). For compatibilists there can be no such thing as an actual choice. *If you are ultimately determined, there is no fundamental causal difference between physical coercion and any other types of cause, such as social pressure or persuasion. The difference between a gun and social pressure could only be a difference in form, not a difference in causal power. Freedom from coercion is only meaningful if you already possess free will; in that context physical coercion would prevent you from acting on your self-chosen, rational judgment, e.g., as in resisting social pressure.*

- A slightly modified version of compatibilism attempts to get around the desire problem by arguing that free will is responsiveness to reason (which can affect your desires); that you are free to think rationally about your desires. In short, you can deliberate. But there are problems here, too. First, why *responsiveness* to reason, rather than the power to actively regulate one's thinking? This still makes you reactive rather than able to make choices. Second, what makes you responsive to reason? What is the cause of your rational thinking? For compatibilists, there is no answer compatible with free will; there would have to be an ulterior cause of thinking. You would not be able to act differently under the same circumstances.

So here is the problem with compatibilism: you allegedly have choice in some way, but in the end you don't. In the last analysis all your choices are caused by some prior cause. So it doesn't work to say that you are free unless someone is pushing you around or threatening you. Compatibilists are unable to defend the idea that the individual is in some form a causal initiator. To them this implies an uncaused cause. Compatibilists, in the end, cannot support free will.

We will see shortly that one can be the "cause of oneself" in an important respect—without any disregard for and actually based on the law of causality.

## Libertarianism

Philosophical libertarians (not to be confused with political libertarians) claim to sincerely believe in free will; that is, they don't accept the compatibilist view that you can somehow have freedom and determinism at the same time. Many libertarians believe, correctly, that to have free will the individual must possess "agency" or causal power, but they have not shown just what this power consists of. Some get stopped by the argument that such power would necessitate a further cause, which would imply determinism. This pushes some of them toward compatibilism, whether they acknowledge it or not. To escape this dilemma, some libertarians embrace indeterminism. They argue that free will means that some actions are not caused, and that they occur at random or by chance. They often resort to relying on elementary particle theory from physics, which claims that such particles act randomly (Tse 2013, 11).

We have seen in Chapter Two that there can be no randomness in the universe; the law of identity is inescapable, an axiom. But even if metaphysical randomness existed, that idea would not help the libertarians.

Many critics have pointed out the obvious: if your alleged choices are random (uncaused), then it means you have no control over them. You are simply a leaf blowing in the wind. A lack of determinism is not the same as self-regulated choice.

*The prevalent belief that we have to choose between determinism and indeterminism is to assume false alternatives.* Clearly, some other approach is needed. There has to be a primary (first cause) and it has to be within the person.

## What Free Will Is

What, then, is the starting point or prime mover within us? (Obviously I am taking automatic, unconscious goal-directed action as a given—as explained in Chapter Three.) The answer has been hinted at throughout the book. Free will is based on the possession of the conceptual faculty, the uniquely human form of consciousness. *The fundamental choice is whether or not to use it, to raise one's level of focus to the conceptual level, the level of rational thought, or to let oneself remain at the automatic, sensory-perceptual level.* "Focus is the state of purposeful alertness of a goal-directed mind committed to attaining full awareness of reality" (Peikoff 1991).[26] To raise one's level of focus to the level of conceptual thought is a choice that requires effort, as does sustaining it.

As a professor for thirty-four years, here is my favorite example. You are assigned reading for a course; the book has material (ideas) you have never seen before. You are sitting on a bench near the lecture hall fifteen minutes before class starts and have opened the textbook in front of you. You hold a highlighter in your hand. You start reading the first sentence in full focus. Then you start thinking: "Whew, this is new. These are long words. I have never read anything like this before. This seems hard." You move down the page and dab the highlighter at some words you have never

---

26   See also Rheins 2016 and Binswanger 2014.

seen, assuming they must be important. But soon your eyes glaze over and all you see is the print on the page. You get to the end of the first page. You realize you do not have the slightest idea of what you just read. You realize you were out of focus, conceptually. You saw the printed words but gained no grasp of their meaning at all. The perception of the print was automatic; the understanding of the words was not. In the end, you did not do any actual thinking. To understand that page, you would have to start reading it all over again and remain in full focus. Everyone I have ever asked has had related experiences, usually many—and not only in reading. One can go "out of focus" about anything.

An addendum to this: for many years, students would come to my office after receiving a low exam grade and claim that they knew the material, but could not recall it during the exam due to anxiety. After much questioning, I discovered that this was not true. The students failed to perform well because they did not know the material, and their anxiety was due to realizing it when confronted with the test questions. These students did not study the material; they simply "re-read" the pages in the text (if that).[27]

Ayn Rand calls the fundamental choice: the choice to think or not to think. There are actually two ways to not think: to remain mentally passive or to deliberately evade.[28] Evasion is the refusal to think about a topic or fact that contradicts what you think or believe or that upsets you; more deeply, it is the refusal to know. It means pushing something you do not want to face out of awareness or not letting it in. It means you expend energy "to create a fog" (Peikoff 1991, 61).

---

27    As a result of this discovery, I wrote a book on how to study: *Study Methods and Study Motivation* 1998.
28    See Binswanger, Peikoff and Rheins for further details.

## Degrees of Focus

Being in conceptual focus is not necessarily all or nothing. There are degrees of focus. I had a graduate student once who had a lot of trouble writing clearly. After some discussion, he admitted that all he tried to do was "to get a rough idea" of the ideas or concepts he was talking about. But his focus was always partly fuzzy, so he never achieved full clarity. He was sort of half-focused and thus routinely only half understood what he was writing about. Focus is a continuum, ranging from barely above the perceptual level to half grasping concepts to full conceptual awareness. A useful metaphor is to think of the conceptual faculty as controlled by one's own dimmer switch. One can have a dim focus on something but can adjust the degree of focus anywhere between dim and bright. One can go up and down. Dim would mean being vaguely aware of something, a blurry idea in a darkened corner somewhere. At any time one has the power to adjust the dimmer switch. If one does not adjust it, the default setting is low because focus requires effort.

One can, then, drift mindlessly, but in a certain respect a human being cannot totally escape the conceptual level unless in a stupor. A child starts learning about object concepts (ball, pillow, teddy bear) at an early age and moves on from there to concepts of attributes and higher level abstractions (animal, flower, sit, run, arithmetic, parts of speech, etc.) As one grows and learns, these concepts are stored in the subconscious and come into play automatically as needed (e.g., during speaking, conversing, or studying). At some level every person is aware that that they can go out of focus and come back into focus. Even if one is passive, the mind will not stay empty; the subconscious will feed you non-purposeful associations. But one has the power (through introspection, which is volitional focus directed inwards, at one's own mental processes) to detect when they are drifting down and move back up.

## Self-Causation

Of course, determinists (and indeterminists) will ask at this point: well, what causes you to think, to use reason? The answer is: you are the cause. *The choice to think or not is self-caused, a volitionally chosen primary. This is not a denial of the law of causality but a specific form of it, a form found in human beings who possess the rational faculty.* Like consciousness as such, which is an emergent property of a certain type of brain and nervous system, free will (volition) is an emergent property of a brain that makes possible a conceptual (rational) consciousness. Your choice is whether to use your free will or not. Volitional causality is different from mechanical causality. Thoughts have different attributes than physical entities (Chapter Two). You can choose differently under the same circumstances. This does not violate the law of identity but reflects it. Human consciousness, like everything else, has a nature.

It should be clear from the above and Chapter Two that this version of free will, which is from Ayn Rand (Peikoff 1991), is not reductionism (materialism), not idealism (only ideas exist), not double aspect theory, not randomness, and not dualism (in the sense of a mind as an entity totally separate from the brain). Emergence is the best label I can come up with (and was used in Chapter 2 in reference to the concept of consciousness itself). As noted previously, the concept of emergence as such is even applicable to the material world. It refers to the fact that when atoms or molecules combine into a new existent, new capacities for action emerge. For example, water is an emergent property of a certain combination of hydrogen and oxygen. In biological organisms, emergence is ubiquitous. Emergence is not an original idea. (Emergentism is a specialized field with its own internal disputes that are beyond the scope of this book.) The basic idea goes back to the ancient Greeks and, as noted, is implicit if not explicit in all science. It applies to both animate and inanimate existents.

One can ask further: why is the choice to focus a primary (Peikoff, 1991)? For example, isn't it the result of deliberation? No; you have some degree of focus before you can deliberate. Isn't it caused by our values? But you have to choose to think; to turn on your conceptual faculty in order to choose values, be aware of values, and decide to act on them. What about rewards? You have to think in order to decide that something is rewarding to you (because of your values) and then you have to think in order to figure out how to attain them. What about social pressure? As noted in Chapter Four, people's minds are not physically interconnected. Other people (assuming no physical coercion) can only express ideas. If you are mentally passive and fail to make any independent judgments about what others say, then you will be a conformist. But you always have the power to question what others tell you. (I am referring to adults; children learn about their power to regulate their thinking gradually.) What about your boss, who has a degree of financial power over you? If you decide you want to do well in your job, you need to accomplish what you are paid for. But you can question your boss's views in your own mind and then decide what actions you need to or are willing to take.

Is there any biological context for the choice to focus? Since thinking is one's main means of survival, the choice to think is, by implication, the choice to live. The choice to abandon the mind is the choice to give up on life.

What aspect of this view of free will is self-evident? The fact that you have to choose to exert the effort required to think. This makes thinking radically different than, though dependent on, the material provided by the senses; the process of sense perception is automatic, unconscious, and effortless. Further, it is obvious that thinking can be wrong. Every belief in your mind is not true. You have to expend effort if you want to gain knowledge by grasping concepts, which includes validating your conceptual conclusions (as noted in the previous chapter).

On the negative side, only this form of free will avoids the contradiction of determinism. It is not that free will is validated negatively. As noted before, it is self-evident. But the problem of self-contradiction dooms any attempt to assert that the conceptual level of functioning is determined by the physical brain or any other causal force other than you making a choice.

People can develop the habit of non-thinking and that makes thinking harder. They can develop the habit of thinking and that makes it easier. But habits are developed by one's choices. Such habits are never fully automatic. Thinking is not sense perception. Focus is not a one-time thing—it is a continual choice one faces every day, all day, throughout the whole of one's life. Of course, people need rest but when and how to rest is also a choice.

## Free Will as Axiomatic

What, then, is the philosophical status of the concept of free will? *It is an axiom, a corollary of the axiom of consciousness, but it applies only to the human form of consciousness. It is an axiom of conceptual knowledge. If free will is an axiom, this has an important implication: free will can neither be proved nor disproved.* Because it is an axiom, free will has to be assumed in any attempt to prove or disprove anything (Peikoff 1991). This means that no research finding could have any bearing on the axiom. It is volitional thinking that controls research and discovers knowledge. Any claim by a neuroscientist that they have found proof of determinism would involve a hopeless contradiction, viz. "I have found experimental proof that all beliefs and conclusions, including my own, are caused by forces beyond my, or anyone's, control." How could they know that?

I want to repeat what I said in Chapter Two about how one validates (not proves) axioms. The primary axioms (existence, identity, and consciousness) are axioms because: (1) they are self-evident to perception (implicit even in one's first experiences); (2) they are the required base of all subsequent knowledge; (3) one has to use them even in the process of trying to refute them (Peikoff 1991). These are not actually three separate arguments but the same idea from three different perspectives. The axiom of free will is implicit in the axiom of a consciousness that is conceptual.

Free will presumably develops in children as they develop their conceptual faculty, perhaps starting with the choice to pay attention.

*If free will is an axiom, then it is neither an illusion nor, as some argue, a "necessary" illusion. Rather, it is determinism that is illusory. Nothing can be true that violates an axiom and thus entails a self-contradiction.* (Epicurus noted this contradiction over 2000 years ago but almost no one got the message.)

## Is There Freedom of Action?

Free will theorists have primarily focused their discussion of free will on the regulation of action. There is a respect in which this is true, but it is incomplete. One cannot talk about freedom of action without reference to the mind. Peikoff writes, "In the realm of physical action, man's choice is twofold. First he must choose, through a process of thought (or non-thought) [passive conformity] the ideas and values that will comprise his mind's content. Then he must choose to act on these ideas and values— to keep them operative as a guide amid all the vicissitudes of daily life." (Peikoff 1991, 67-68). The choice to think is the base for other choices. Purposeful action requires one to choose one's goals and values and the means to attain them. One needs to keep focused on what one wants and then choose to take the needed action. One's thinking needs to be applied to the specific issue or circumstance at hand at the time of action. The failure to act on one's values can be the result of not paying attention, or of having conflicting value judgments, or of not formulating a clear value hierarchy, or of giving into an emotion, or of not wanting to exert mental effort. When one is not in full focus the subconscious takes over by default, based on whatever impulses one has at the time of action. But even then one can choose to act or not to act on the impulse.

Consider these two student scenarios (condensed from Binswanger 2014, 334-336):

First student's thoughts:

Am I going to study tonight, or watch TV? I guess I ought to study—but that course—ugh! Professor Winston is so boring. I don't see why I should have to force myself to study something if the teacher cannot make it interesting. He wants us to do all the work while all he does is read his lectures from a script... .He's probably watching TV right now. What's on TV tonight? Oh, that great old Bogart film. That's the one I saw last year with Maureen. I remember how she cried at the end of the film. That was really nice. Maureen is nice. I don't know why I didn't pursue a relationship with her. Hey, I could ask her over right now to watch that movie on TV. Repeating our old date—that would come across as real romantic.

Oh, but what about the final? Aw, I guess I'm prepared enough, and   everyone knows you can bluff your way through philosophy tests. [He reaches for the phone.]

Second student's thoughts:

Am I going to study tonight or watch TV? What's at stake? My grade-point average. If I don't do well on the final tomorrow, I'm going to get a C in the course, and that's not going to look too good when I apply to graduate school. But is studying tonight really going to make a difference to my grade? Well, how well do I already understand the material this exam will cover? Well, what will it cover? Oh yeah, Professor Winston said it will be mainly on Aristotle's ethics. What are the topics of Aristotle's ethics that we are going to be responsible for? [Looks at his notes.]....

Okay, if I'm hazy on... [Aristotle's view of happiness], I'm not going to do too well. Winston's hinted more than once that Aristotle's view of happiness is important. I could re-read my notes on happiness and check a secondary source.

But then that's going to take time, and that great Bogart film is on TV tonight. I'd hate to miss it. And after all, I'm entitled to some pleasure in life. No, that's just an excuse. Could I even enjoy the movie, with tomorrow's exam looming over me? No, I really, really want to get into a good grad school; my whole future depends on that.

But I do want to see that movie! Do I have to miss it? Is there some other way? Wait—it must be out as a video. Yeah, I'll rent [download, live stream] the video tomorrow night after the exam as a reward for nailing down Aristotle's view of happiness tonight. [He reaches for his study materials.]

Observe that both students were in conflict. But the first student indulged their feelings and wishes, blamed the teacher for the problem, and rationalized the failure to prepare better. The second student also had a wish, but stopped rationalizing and blaming the teacher for their problem. The student identified the connection between the exam and long range goals and postponed gratification. The first student was wish-focused, the second reality-focused. This led to different actions.

Now consider a more mundane example, but one that is quite popular in the free will literature. Can I raise my hand if I want to? The answer is yes, but there is a cognitive context here, too. Why would I want to? There could be many reasons: to prove I can (e.g., to thumb my nose at determinists); to interrupt a conversation; to catch a waiter's attention; to ask a question after a presentation; to stretch a sore shoulder muscle, etc. One has a motive and can choose to act on it or not.

When would someone decide not to raise a hand? Perhaps due to fear of embarrassment, fear of being thought rude, or fear of being verbally and physically attacked. Again, one can choose to act or not to act on the motive.

This does not mean that the cognitive context itself reflects determinism. Things get into your subconscious originally via the conscious mind. The reason that freedom of action may seem direct is that our subconscious is a storehouse that operates automatically, and in many situations deliberation before action is not needed (Chapter 2). For example, habitual actions such a taking a shower in the morning, going to work, or making coffee have already been appraised as appropriate and all the conscious mind needs to do is to set the actions in motion.

But many actions do require deliberation. Let's say that you have been dishonest from some time and after some thought, you have decided to be an honest person and have thought the issue through clearly. But to become honest, you must act in an honest fashion every day, all day. To remain honest over time, you must consciously hold in mind the virtue you want to practice when deciding how to act. People have the power to program their subconscious through thought and repeated actions so that the types of actions they consciously desire become almost second nature; but they are never fully automatic. It is possible to slip up. You may forget your goal in the heat of the moment or may want to escape the consequences of some mistaken or irrational action. You may be afraid or in conflict. You may temporarily go out of focus. People can act without thinking and let the emotion of the moment take over. But, people also have the ability to identify what they are thinking and doing and reassert their moral compass. A person who has acquired the habit of consistent irrationality will find developing new rational habits to be very difficult (Locke and Dennis 2012).

To summarize, people know through introspection that they have the power to go in and out of conceptual focus, to let their minds drift passively, to be half in focus, or to strive for full conceptual clarity. They can choose to think some of the time and not others. They can give into the emotions of the moment or try to understand them. They can refuse to think about an issue that is unpleasant or face it head-on. They can choose to learn more or stagnate. This choice is open to people all day, everyday (illness and disability aside—see below).

# What Free Will Can and Cannot Do

### Potency but not Omnipotence

Reason is our main means of survival (see Chapter Two). But the fact that you can choose to think does not mean that you can achieve anything you want. People like to say that with effort, persistence, and a positive attitude you can achieve anything. The spirit of such an attitude is admirable and very American, but it cannot be taken literally. If you have no voice, you cannot become an opera star. If you are not coordinated, you cannot become a world class athlete. If you can barely understand arithmetic, you are unlikely to become a scientific genius. (Cognitive ability is discussed below.) Any number of factors can cause someone to fail to attain an intended goal despite their best efforts (e.g., lack of skill or ability, age or infirmity, illness, fatigue, lack of knowledge, lack of commitment, conflict, interference from nature or other people, etc.). Successful action is conditional.

This is not to say that, guided by thought, you cannot work to improve or try to overcome past failures. Everyone can learn. They can improve over where they started with respect to any skill. But everyone will not get to the same place. The much popularized claim by Ericcson, Krampe and Tesch-Romer (1991) that, for example, with 10,000 hours of practice anyone can become world class—such as playing the violin—cannot be taken seriously. Everyone does not have the same musical capacity. In sports, some studies show that deliberate practice only accounts for 1% of the variation in performance (Macnamara, Moreau, and Hambrick 2016; Macnamara, Hambrick, and Moreau 2016), although this figure is probably substantially on the low side for most skills. All you can say is that you will almost certainly get better at anything you try with practice. Does this mean you should just give up if you are not born with "star" potential? No. This is not the way to come at life. You cannot know your future potential when you start out because you have not attempted anything. You learn your limits by simply trying stuff. Feel free to get expert advice, but don't let anyone tell you what you can achieve if you have good reason to disagree. In the end, if you exert effort, reality gives you feedback about what you can and cannot accomplish. For example, if you cannot sing, you will not be able to get any singing jobs. If you cannot do math, you will not be admitted to an engineering program. If you are uncoordinated, forget about a professional career in tennis. But by using your mind to the fullest, you have the best chance to actualize whatever potential you might have.

Special mention must be made of mental illness. This malady, of which there are many varieties, is usually due to problems with your brain. Your brain is your hardware (Chapter One); if it is damaged, it affects your cognitive (and especially your conceptual) capacity as well as your emotions. The causes include heredity (e.g., genetic abnormality), physical and mental trauma, disease, and aging. Your own actions can cause brain and bodily damage, such as drug abuse and lifestyle (diet, lack of exercise, smoking, etc.). Of course, thinking problems can be caused by your own lack of prior thinking. Brain problems characteristically undercut your ability to think and they affect your emotional state to varying degrees. Some problems, including addiction, may be reversible or treatable and others not, based on our current knowledge of the brain. Further, the way you think and what you think can actually change your brain (Volk 2013).[29] Using your mind to its fullest extent can be of enormous help in dealing with mental illness, but it cannot cure everything. (How to decide when a person is legally responsible for their actions when mentally ill or possessing extremely low intellectual ability is beyond the scope of this book.)

A note about free will and living in a dictatorship: dictators rule by physical coercion and the inculcation of fear by threat. What power does the victim have? A dictator cannot control whether you think or not. But they can try to limit what information is available to you via censorship. Dictators can limit what you say publically and how you act in public (e.g.,

---

29   Volk discusses the research of Dr. Jeffrey Schwartz, who treats patients with OCD.

preventing you from organizing a peaceful protest) through threats of imprisonment, torture, or death.

Dictators can propagandize via control of the media. Free will, however, still gives one the ability to identify contradictions. Here are some examples:

- The dictator says everyone is living well but there is mass starvation.

- The dictator says there is freedom of speech but people who criticize him are arrested, imprisoned, or killed.

- The dictator says there are free elections, but it is a one party system and virtually no one who opposes it is ever elected or can even run for office (and may be killed).

- The dictator says there is justice, but the courts are totally controlled by the state and trials are not open to the public.

- The dictator says every problem in the country is caused by the CIA, when it is obvious that the problems are caused by his own policies (i.e., lawlessness or the destruction of the economy).

It is sometimes possible for victims of dictatorship to obtain information from sources other than the government (internet, books, reports by travelers and foreigners, letters) which characteristically contradict almost everything the dictator says. Victims can engage in secret rebellion, of course, but at great personal risk. They can also try to escape, also at great risk (e.g., note the mass attempts to escape from repressive states where for many life has no chance).

## Knowledge but not Omniscience

I have noted—and everyone already knows—that thinking is fallible. We are not born with any knowledge; it has to be acquired. There is no guarantee of success. Conceptual knowledge does not come pre-packaged in the form of revelations, nor is knowledge a matter of public consensus.

Agreement is not a method of knowing and is not a method of science. Discovering knowledge requires use of the senses and reason which includes the use of conceptual tools such as mathematics and physical instruments discovered or invented through thinking.

Rational agreement comes after one or more scientists has presented convincing evidence and resistance, if any, has been overcome or has faded away. Accumulating evidence and convincing doubters can take a long time and enormous effort by many people. It took some 1,500 years (from the ancient Greeks) to prove that the earth circles the sun and not the other way around, and to get the idea accepted. It took another 1,500 years to discover the germ theory of disease and have it prevail in medical practice. And so on with millions of other discoveries. General acceptance eventually follows the evidence among those who respect reason, look at the evidence, and find it compelling.

## Indirect but not Direct Control Over Emotions

Introspection—a critical method of psychology that is virtually forbidden in scientific reports—reveals that emotions are not directly willed but are automatic (Locke 2009). How does emotion work? (I am leaving out brain abnormalities in this discussion.) This was discussed briefly in Chapter Two.[30] The process, in the simplest terms, is: object—appraisal—emotion. The object can be anything one can perceive or be aware of, including a person, action, object, idea, or a prior emotion. The appraisal is subconscious and has two aspects. There is a cognitive appraisal which connects the object to stored knowledge, viz. what is this, what are its attributes? What's going on? There is a corresponding value appraisal: what does this mean to me given my values? *Emotions are the form in which one experiences automatic, subconscious appraisals of existents (including*

---

30  For details see Locke's article in the *Handbook of Principles of Organizational Behavior* 2009.

*ideas).* Every emotion has a unique type of subconscious appraisal. Fear is the form in which one experiences threat. Anger involves the appraisal of injustice. Jealousy involves the appraisal of someone having an attribute or value that you would like to have. Pride results from believing that one has attained something important or valuable through one's own efforts. Satisfaction comes from concluding that one has what one wants. Love is the result of appraising another person as a great personal value. What one consciously experiences is: object—emotion. The appraisals are discovered after the fact by introspecting backwards. The survival value of emotional automation is obvious. A cave man who went into deep thinking about the nature of the saber tooth tigers on the trail ahead before running would not live very long. Emotions include felt action tendencies such as approach, attack, avoid, protect, etc. Emotions (except perhaps depression, which undermines the desire to act) energize us. Emotions make our values psychologically "real"; without them our values would be experienced as dry abstractions devoid of any motivation to act.

It has been claimed by some psychologists that perception leads to action and then to emotion (e.g., bear, run, fear). This order is just wrong. Why would one run unless there was some appraisal of danger? What may confuse people is that the cognitive and value appraisals, being automatic, are lightning fast. The emotional response and the accompanying tendency to flee occur almost simultaneously with the appraisal. Nonetheless, as I noted earlier, people do not act without some prior cognitive context. Putting action before any context would make it causeless.

It is easy to verify the appraisal view of emotions through mental experiments and even classroom demonstrations. For a mental experiment, imagine you were deep in the woods with no weapon and were confronted by a charging grizzly bear. You would feel fear. Now imagine that you were watching the same charge from inside a strong glass enclosure in the same woods. There would be far less fear because the appraisal would be benign; the bear would not be a threat in that context. For a classroom demonstration, consider what I used to do in introductory psychology classes. Part way through a lecture, I would say (falsely) that there was going to be an unannounced quiz right then and that it would count toward the students' grades. I would then have teaching assistants get up carrying sheaves of paper, and pretend they were about to hand out the quizzes. There was agonized murmuring. I would then admit it was all fake, and asked students to tell me what emotions they had just been feeling. It was always two things: anger, because the unannounced quiz was seen as unfair, and anxiety, because they felt they would perform poorly—which would threaten their grades. When I revealed the truth, the emotions immediately subsided. Emotions are caused by subconscious ideas.

The fact that emotions are automatic does not make us helpless victims of emotions. We can affect emotional responses indirectly in three different ways—all of which are implicit in the model.

1. **We can work to change the object.**

   For example, if we received a bad grade on an exam and felt depressed, we might not be able to get the grade changed, but we could diagnose our failure and make a plan to do better which would produce a more positive emotion. Similarly, we can work to connect more effectively with a loved one after a lover's spat and improve the relationship (Locke and Kenner 2011).

2. **We can work to change any mistaken, stored beliefs about the object.**

   For example, Mr. A felt very guilty about masturbating. When asked why, he said that a real man should be able to get sex whenever he wanted it. When this mistaken belief was corrected, he experienced immediate relief. Ms. B became depressed when she received a poor grade in an introductory psychology exam. She concluded that it would ruin her course grade, which would ruin her grade average, which would ruin her ability to get into medical school, which would destroy her career goal, which would ruin her life. When this false chain of reasoning was exposed, the depression disappeared. Changing beliefs is not always easy, because they may be connected to other beliefs, including some buried deep in the subconscious. Thus change may take time. Implicit beliefs (e.g., "I am no good") based on early childhood trauma may not be fully curable based on our present knowledge.

3. **We can question, adapt, or change our value standards.** Expecting ourselves to be omnipotent or omniscient will lead to constant self-belittlement and self-doubt and often to the use of elaborate defensive maneuvers. Irrational goals (e.g., "I have to please everyone;" "I have no right to my own happiness because I must live to sacrifice;" "Pride is a sin so I must feel work to devalue my achievements") cannot be attained without harming one's well-being. Unhealthy values need to be replaced with healthy ones. Again, value systems may be deeply automatized and change may take a long time or be almost impossible (based on current knowledge), if set at a very early age. Of course, as they grow, many people change and revise their value systems or specific values all the time. Most children do not end up exactly like their parents.

Emotions do not have to be acted upon, even though they contain action tendencies or impulses. This is true even in the face of danger. Suppose you are hiking on the African plains and come across a cheetah. You might have previously learned that cheetahs like to pursue from behind and are extremely fast. In this case you might override your initial desire to run and decide to stand facing it and hope for the best. (Good luck!) In social situations, one can decide that a contemplated and desired action is inappropriate, based on your wider context of knowledge and total value system. One might be angry at an injustice and temporarily feel the desire to harm the perceived perpetrator, but then decide that such action would be morally wrong or harmful to oneself. One is free to think of action alternatives. Those who start to act immediately on impulse at an early age without learning limits may develop dangerous habits and put themselves (and others) at risk in every aspect of their lives, unless the habit is corrected.

It must be noted that emotions can be deliberately suppressed—that is, pushed out of awareness even though they (and their causes) still exist. Sometimes this is necessary in order to attend to some pressing matter, but continual suppression can cause emotional stultification. Emotions can also be repressed: kept out of awareness by a screening order ("I must not feel anger at my mother"), even though they still exist in the subconscious. Refusing to allow awareness does not make emotions go away. This can have unfortunate psychological consequences, such as blocking the motivational power of emotions in general and preventing cognitive integration. The volitional alternative is to try to consciously identify the emotion and its causes so that one can take steps to achieve emotional well-being.

The bottom line here is that, although emotions are automatic and subconsciously powered, many volitional processes involving emotions are possible: identifying them, discovering their causes, taking new actions, reprogramming, and, for better or for worse, trying to keep them out of awareness. (As noted, some emotional problems can be caused by brain or hormonal issues which may require special treatment and/or therapy.)

## Volition is Real but It May be Hard to Focus at Certain Times

There are times when choosing to think is much harder than at other times or may be temporarily impossible. Some obvious examples are being fatigued, ill, extremely stressed, or injured. Human beings are not disembodied minds divorced from the world. But even in difficult circumstances some thinking may be possible: I need to rest, I need to see a doctor (or take my medications), I need to figure out what's causing the stress and develop a plan of action, I need to modify how I live, etc.

## Not Related to Entropy

Some commentators who have studied science claim that free will would violate the second law of thermodynamics in physics. This law says that in a closed system, if heat is introduced, it will spread out until the temperature is equal throughout. This process involves an increase in entropy, which is defined as an increase in disorder. However, disorder in this context has a technical, statistical meaning which has nothing to do with what you and I mean by disorder or chaos. Air molecules behave in a lawful fashion. I fail to see any connection here to free will. Humans have the power to mobilize mental and physical energy to think and to pursue values.

## Helps you to Act Smarter but is not the Same as Intelligence

Intelligence, sometimes called cognitive ability, is the capacity to grasp abstractions (concepts). General intelligence is called the "G" factor. People with high intelligence simply "get" concepts better and faster and can proceed to grasp higher levels of abstraction than those with less intelligence. Intelligence has a significant genetic component. There is debate over how to what degree intelligence is hereditary, but most experts claim it is between 50% and 80%. Many scientists don't like (and often evade) this concept, because it means everyone is not equal in ultimate capacity. We have to accept that fact that people differ (even when they all exert the same effort). One cannot gain anything by revolting against the facts of reality. But all this does not mean that intelligence is everything. *Innate cognitive capacity is only a potential.* Actualizing it involves many factors. No one would dispute that environmental factors, of which they are many (e.g., nutrition, home environment, education, mentors, freedom from violence etc.) are important. But volition is important too which involves dedication to thinking. Within limits, you can make yourself more intelligent by making full use of your rational faculty. I like the widely used metaphor of the brain as a muscle: the more you use it the stronger it gets. (Again, this does not mean that everyone ends up the same.)

Rational thinking, the exercise of free will, and utilizing whatever intellectual ability you have will make a huge difference in your life. Consider how persistence and constant learning can improve your life even if cognitive ability is limited. On the other side of the coin, imagine a smart person who is irrational, dishonest, and lazy—where will they end up? Undoubtedly somewhere bad. Because they are smart they will have a lot of ideas; because they are irrational, none of them will work (none will be tied to reality and their objective needs). Their intelligence might work against them; they might think they are smart enough to get away with crime. The key to success is developing and using whatever cognitive potential you have, and making the most of it by using reason to constantly learn and guide your choices and actions.[31] Prospering is a learned skill.

## Not the Only Factor in Attention

Free will allows you to be in focus and thus allows you to choose what to attend to (i.e., things you value). But not everything you pay attention to is consciously willed. Certain events are impossible not to notice—e. g., a very loud noise, an accident that you are involved in, a severe pain, a strong smell, a fire in your house, an emergency involving a loved one, an attack by a wild animal, etc. But for most people life is not a series of sudden emergencies. Further, you have the power to discover the cause of the emergency and decide what to do about it.

---

31  Today it is popular in psychology to claim that there are "multiple intelligences." These include: kinesthetic, interpersonal, moral, musical, and emotional intelligence. This idea has been widely criticized because there is no logical (or statistical) connection between the different types. These types are best called skills. I believe that the motive for this multiplication of intelligences is political and not scientific. Putting all these skills under the rubric of intelligence gives them cachet and well as making people seem more equal.

## Not the Same as Mindfulness

Mindfulness has recently become a very popular (even faddish) term, but the more it is used the more muddled the concept has become. It has been used to mean some aspect of Buddhism, focus on emotions, being non-judgmental, meditation, relaxation, awareness of the present, paying attention, non-self-focus, remembering, self-acceptance, and more. A concept with this many different meanings becomes incoherent. Further, none of them seem to refer to raising one's mind to the conceptual level.

## Not intuition

Intuition is not some mysterious or ineffable ability. Intuition is simply an automatic signal from your subconscious involving a judgment or an emotional response. It is based on stored knowledge being called to awareness by some (not necessarily consciously identified) object, attribute, or item of information. Often it involves judging other people. Here is an example. State University was hiring a new professor. Mr. X came with very good recommendations and there seemed to be no negatives in play. He gave a good talk about his research. He was then interviewed by the other professors in the department. Most of the interviews were favorable. But one professor thought something was not quite right; Mr. X did not come across as genuine. It was as though he were hiding some part of himself. His emotional responses seemed muted or artificial. It was a red flag, but the professor couldn't put his finger on what was wrong and did not have any objective evidence to vote against him. So Mr. X got the job. Tragedy followed. Mr. X was a womanizer, a liar, and he seemed depressed. Some faculty members took him to the counseling center, but he lied to the counselor. He was a drug addict. After being suspended for seducing students (one of whom went to the Dean), he soon committed suicide by drug overdose. His former advisors knew nothing of Mr. X's total self. His former fellow graduate students did know something, but student peers are not asked for letters of recommendation. Later it was learned that a second faculty member also thought something was off, but he also couldn't figure out what. In this case, the two negative intuitions were correct, but they couldn't be validated ahead of hiring.

Sometimes intuitions are correct, as with Mr. X, but at other times they are not ("Hey, I have a feeling that Flying Spurs is going to win the Kentucky Derby!"—and he comes in last). The challenge is to consciously identify what set off the positive or negative reaction(s). Intuitions are not knowledge; they are best viewed as hypotheses. They need validation, which can be very challenging. How to do this is outside the scope of this book, but the starting point is always gathering more information. This is where volition comes in.

## Not Just for Resisting Temptation

Religion stresses using will power to resist temptation, but this is unfortunate on three counts. First, if temptation involves breaking a strongly established habit (e.g., smoking or overeating) direct will power will not necessarily work because the problem is too automatized. Such habits are more likely to be changed indirectly, by going through a process or stages, often with outside help. Even with help success is not guaranteed (Locke and Dennis 2012). Second, the focus on the negative aspects of temptation is far too narrow. The function of the mind is gaining knowledge, choosing values, and then directing one's life. This includes attaining positives through goal-directed action. Third, if temptation involves doing something unethical, it usually means that the individual lacks strong values or has a value conflict. One can try to suppress the conflict, but a better course of action is to identify the source of the conflict and to bring one's value system into conscious awareness.

## Cannot Create all of Oneself

It has been said by some philosophers that free will is impossible because one cannot be the "cause of oneself." Physically this is, on the whole, true. One cannot choose one's own body and brain though one can take steps to make them better. (Gene replacement may be possible sometime in the future). However, one can create one's own soul, starting with a process of thought and then choosing one's values and goals and acting to attain them (see Chapter Four). This includes developing one's knowledge and skills, building one's moral character, choosing one's own friends, choosing the situations one enters into (in a free country), changing situations to suit one's needs, looking for opportunity and long-range thinking (Locke in press).

# 9

# CONCLUDING REMARKS

Disputing the false assertions made by determinists listed in the introduction, I have worked to show that:

- Consciousness is axiomatic but it not material but rather an emergent property of the brain;

- Conscious thought is critical to human survival.

- The human mind, due to evolution, is radically more advanced and life-enhancing than the chimpanzee mind, not to mention other species; the conceptual level is an enormous advance over the sensory-perceptual level.

- Causality is universal and pertains to the actions of existents based on the law of identity; probability is not the result of indeterminism but of limited knowledge. All causes are not material. Consciousness has identity and is causal but does not operate by mechanical principles.

- Goal-directedness applies only to the actions of living organisms and exists at different levels, from unconscious to perceptual to volitional.

- The self is a valid concept and starts with the awareness that one is conscious.

- The neuroscience experiments alleged to prove determinism prove no such thing.

- Determinism is a self-contradictory doctrine and makes objective knowledge impossible, including knowledge of determinism.

- Free will is an axiom of conceptual knowledge and precedes any attempt to prove (or disprove) anything; it is determinism rather than free will that is an illusion.

- Free will is not based on randomness but consists of the self-initiated choice to raise one's mental functioning to the conceptual level, which means the choice to think or not to think. Reason is the faculty of volition.

Why then have the issues of consciousness and free will posed such a problem, given that they are self-evident? There is a certain irony here. People on the street who are attacked for believing in "folk psychology" are basically correct but do not know how to defend their beliefs philosophically, while those with scientific and philosophical knowledge reject the self-evident because they cannot connect it with their own scientific paradigm, which is based on mechanical or material causality. They simply cannot accept that consciousness is sui generis (unique), something different from (even though dependent on) the brain and yet not mystical. Behaviorism (determinism from without) may be dead but a neuroscience model (determinism from within) is vying to take its place; these are but two sides of the same coin.[32]

There is a related factor. Most scientists, including psychologists (or at least those who are not psychotherapists) reject introspection as a scientific method. They may use it in secret and smuggle it in by asking for

---

32  As noted in Chapter Eight, I fully support neuroscience research; it is their often held model of humanity that I find wanting.

subjects' "verbal reports," but you will virtually never see it openly offered as a method of science. In philosophy and psychology this has to be a core method. You need to know what is going on in your own mind and you cannot get there by staring at neurons. You can neither form nor grasp psychological concepts without introspection (Locke 2009, 24-25). The issue of how to validate specific introspective reports is legitimate but beyond the scope of this book. The introspective knowledge required to validate consciousness and volition, being self-evident and being axiomatic, does not require further validation—only identification and explanation.

# REFERENCES

## Preface

Bandura, Albert. "Reconstrual of 'Free Will' from the Agentic Perspective of Social Cognitive Theory." In *Are We Free? Psychology and Free Will*, edited by J. Baer, J. C. Kaufman, and R. F. Baumeister, 86-127. New York: Oxford, 2008.

Frede, Michael. *A Free Will: Origins of the Notion in Ancient Thought*. Berkeley: University of California Press, 2011.

Graffin, G. W., and W. P. Provine. "Evolution, Religion and Free Will." *American Scientist* 95, no. 4 (July-August 2007): 294-97.

Pereboom, Derk, ed. *Free Will*. 2nd ed. Indianapolis: Hackett Publishing Company, Inc., 2009.

## Chapter Two

Binswanger, Harry, ed. *Ayn Rand Lexicon*. New York: New American Library, 1986.

Edelman, Gerald M., and Giulio Tononi. *A Universe of Consciousness: How Matter Becomes Imagination*. New York: Basic Books, 2000.

Gazzaniga, Michael. *Who's in Charge?: Free Will and the Science of the Brain*. New York: Ecco, 2011.

Ghate, Onkar. "Postmodernism's Kantian Roots." In *Postmodernism in Management: Pros, Cons and the Alternative*, edited by Edwin A. Locke. Amsterdam: JAI Press, 2003.

Herman, A. *The Cave and the Light*. New York: Random House, 2014.

Locke, Edwin A. "Attain Emotional Control by Understanding What Emotions Are." In *Handbook of Principles of Organizational Behavior*. 2nd ed. New York: Wiley, 2009.

Locke, Edwin A. and John Dennis. "Changing Habits: Why It's Hard, How to Do It." Course presented at the Objectivist Summer Conference, San Diego, CA, July 2012.

Peikoff, Leonard. *Objectivism: The Philosophy of Ayn Rand*. New York: Dutton, 1991.

Peikoff, Leonard. *The Dim Hypothesis*. New York: New American Library, 2012.

Rand, Ayn. *For the New Intellectual*. New York: Random House, 1961.

Rand, Ayn. "The Stimulus…and the Response." *The Ayn Rand Letter* 1, no. 9 (January 1972) and 1, no. 10 (February 1972).

Rand, Ayn. *Introduction to Objectivist Epistemology*. 2nd ed. New York: New American Library, 1990.

Skinner, B.F. *Beyond Freedom and Dignity*. New York: Knopf, 1971.

Terrace, H. *Nim*. New York: Knopf, 1979.

Wegner, Daniel. *The Illusion of Conscious Will*. Cambridge: MIT Press, 2002.

## Chapter Three

Binswanger, Harry, ed. *Ayn Rand Lexicon*. New York: New American Library, 1986.

Gray, Theodore. *Molecules: The Elements and the Architecture of Everything*. New York: Black Dog and Leventhal, 2014.

Harriman, David. *The Logical Leap*. New York: New American Library, 2010.

Hawking, Stephen. *A Brief History of Time*. Updated and expanded edition. New York: Bantam, 1996.

Peikoff, Leonard. *Objectivism: The Philosophy of Ayn Rand*. New York: Dutton, 1991.

Rand, Ayn. *Introduction to Objectivist Epistemology*. 2nd ed. New York: New American Library, 1990.

Samenow, Stanton. *Inside the Criminal Mind*. New York: Crown, 2004.

Wegner, Daniel. *The Illusion of Conscious Will*. Cambridge: MIT Press, 2002.

## Chapter Four

Binswanger, Harry. "The Goal-Directedness of Living Action." *The Objectivist Forum* 7, no. 4 (1986): 4-5.

Binswanger, Harry. *The Biological Basis of Teleological Concepts*. Marina del Rey: ARI Press, 1990.

Bandura, Albert. *Self-efficacy: The Exercise of Control*. New York: Freeman, 1997.

Deacon, T.W. *Incomplete Nature*. New York: Norton, 2012.

Locke, Edwin A. and G. P. Latham. *A Theory of Goal Setting and Task Performance*. New York: Prentice Hall,1990.

Locke, Edwin A. "Attain Emotional Control by Understanding What Emotions Are." In *Handbook of Principles of Organizational Behavior*. 2nd ed. New York: Wiley, 2009.

Peikoff, Leonard. *The Cause of Hitler's Germany*. New York: Penguin, 1982.

Peikoff, Leonard. *Objectivism: The Philosophy of Ayn Rand*. New York: Dutton, 1991.

Rand, Ayn. *The Virtue of Selfishness*. New York: Signet, 1964.

Seligman, Martin E. P., Peter Railton, Roy F. Baumeister, and Chandra Sripada. "Navigating into the Future or Driven by the Past." *Perspectives on Psychological Science*, 8, no. 2 (2013): 119-141.

## Chapter Five

Bandura, Albert. *Self-efficacy: The Exercise of Control*. New York: Freeman, 1997.

Binswanger, Harry, ed. *Ayn Rand Lexicon*. New York: New American Library, 1986.

Deacon, T.W. *Incomplete Nature*. New York: Norton, 2012.

Johnson, Steven. *How We Got to Now: Six Innovations That Made the Modern World*. New York: Riverhead Books, 2014.

Locke, Edwin A. "The Educational, Psychological, and Philosophical Assault on Self-Esteem." *The Objective Standard* 1, no. 4 (2006-7): 6-82.

Locke, Edwin. A. "Attain Emotional Control by Understanding What Emotions Are." In *Handbook of Principles of Organizational Behavior*. 2nd ed. New York: Wiley, 2009.

Locke, Edwin A. and Ellen Kenner. *The Selfish Path to Romance*. Doylestown: Platform Press, 2011.

Orth, U., and R. W. Robins. "The Development of Self Esteem." *Current Directions in Psychological Science* 23, no. 5 (2014): 381-387.

Rand, Ayn. *The Fountainhead*. New York: Bobs-Merrill, 1943.

Rand, Ayn. *Introduction to Objectivist Epistemology*. 2nd ed. New York: New American Library, 1990.

Samenow, Stanton. *Inside the Criminal Mind*. New York: Crown, 2004.

Strohminger, Nina, Knobe, J. and Newman, J. "The True Self: A Psychological Concept Distinct from the Self" *Perspectives in Psychological Science*, 12, (2017): 551-560.

Wegner, Daniel. *The Illusion of Conscious Will*. Cambridge: MIT Press, 2002.

## Chapter Six

Bandura, Albert. "Reconstrual of 'Free Will' from the Agentic Perspective of Social Cognitive Theory." In *Are We Free? Psychology and Free Will*, edited by J. Baer, J. C. Kaufman, and R. F. Baumeister, 86-127. New York: Oxford, 2008.

Bargh, J. A., and T. L. Chartrand. "The Unbearable Automaticity of Being." *American Psychologist* 54 (1999): 462.

Bode, S., A.H. He, C.S. Soon, R. Trampel, R. Turner, and J-D. Haynes. "Tracking the Unconscious Generation of Free Decisions Using Ultra-High Field fMRI." *Plos One* 6, no. 6 (2011): 1-13.

Bode, S., C. Murawski, C. S. Soon, P. Bode, J. Stahl, and P. L. Smith. "Demystifying 'Free Will': The Role of Contextual Information and Evidence Accumulation for Predictive Brain Activity." *Neuroscience and Biobehavioral Reviews* 47 (2014): 636-45.

Libet, B. "Unconscious Cerebral Initiative and the Role of Conscious Will in Voluntary Action." *Behavioral and Brain Sciences*, 8 (1985): 529-66.

Locke, Edwin A. and G. P. Latham. *A Theory of Goal Setting and Task Performance*. New York: Prentice Hall, 1990.

Locke, Edwin A. and G. P. Latham, eds. *New Developments in Goal Setting and Task Performance*. New York: Routledge, 2013.

Locke, Edwin A. "Theory Building, Replication, and Behavioral Priming: Where do We Go From Here?" *Perspectives on Psychological Science*, 10, no. 3 (2015): 408-14.

Mele, A.R. "Free Will and Science." In *The Oxford Handbook of Free Will*, edited by R. Kane. 2nd ed. Oxford: Oxford Press, 2011.

Oettingen, G., M. Wittchen, and P. M. Gollwitzer. "Regulating Goal Pursuit Through Mental Contrasting and Implementation Intentions." In *New Developments in Goal Setting and Task Performance*, edited by Edwin A. Locke and G. P. Latham. New York: Routledge, 2013.

Soon, C.S., M. Brass, H-J. Heinze, and J-D. Haynes. "Unconscious Determinants of Free Decisions in the Human Brain." *Nature Neuroscience*, 11, no. 5 (2008): 543-45.

Sprang, R. N., and B. Levine. "Doing What We Imagine: Completion Rates and Frequency Attributes of Imagined Future Events One Year After Prospection." *Memory* 21 (2013): 458-66.

## Chapter Seven

Binswanger, Harry. *How We Know: Epistemology on an Objectivist Foundation*. New York: TOF Publications, 2014.

Hawking, Stephen. *A Brief History of Time*. Updated and expanded edition. New York: Bantam, 1996.

Peikoff, Leonard. *Objectivism: The Philosophy of Ayn Rand.* New York: Dutton, 1991.

Wegner, Daniel. *The Illusion of Conscious Will.* Cambridge: MIT Press, 2002.

## Chapter Eight

Binswanger, Harry. *How We Know: Epistemology on an Objectivist Foundation.* New York: TOF Publications, 2014.

Ericcson, Anders, R.T Krampe,. and C. Tesch-Romer. "The role of deliberate practice in the acquisition of expert performance." Psychological Review 100 (1993): 363-406.

Kane, R. *The Oxford Handbook of Free Will.* 2nd ed. Oxford: Oxford Press, 2011.

Locke, Edwin A. *Study Methods and Study Motivation.* New Milford: Second Renaissance Books, 1998.

Locke, Edwin A. "Attain Emotional Control by Understanding What Emotions Are." In *Handbook of Principles of Organizational Behavior.* 2nd ed. New York: Wiley, 2009.

Locke, Edwin A. "It's Time We Brought Introspection Out of the Closet." *Perspectives on Psychological Science* 4, no. 1 (2009): 24-25.

Locke, Edwin A. (in press) "Long Range Thinking and Goal Directed Action." To appear in G. Oettingen, A. T. Servincer & P. M. Gollwitzer (Eds.) *The Psychology of Thinking about the Future.* New York: Guilford.

Locke, Edwin A., and Ellen Kenner. *The Selfish Path to Romance.* Doylestown: Platform Press, 2011.

Locke, Edwin A., and John Dennis. "Changing Habits: Why It's Hard, How to Do It." Course presented at the Objectivist Summer Conference, San Diego, CA, July 2012 . (Available through Ayn Rand Bookstore).

Macnamara, B.N., D. Moreau, and D. Z. Hambrick. " The Relationship Between Deliberate Practice and Performance in Sports: A Meta Analysis." *Perspectives on Psychological Science,* 11, no. 3 (2016): 333-350.

Macnamara, B.N., D. Z. Hambrick, and D. Moreau. "How Important is Deliberate Practice?" *Perspectives on Psychological Science*, 11, no. 3 (2016): 355-358.

Volk, S. "In Defense of Free Will. *Discover*, (November 2013): 51-57.

Peikoff, Leonard. *Objectivism: The Philosophy of Ayn Rand*. New York: Dutton, 1991.

Rheins, J. "The Objectivist Metaphysics." In *A Companion to Ayn Rand*, edited by A. Gotthelf and G. Salmieri. Chichester: Wiley Blackwell, 2016.

Tse, P.U. *The Neural Basis of Free Will*. Cambridge: MIT Press, 2013.

## Chapter Nine

Locke, Edwin A. "It's Time We Brought Introspection Out of the Closet." *Perspectives on Psychological Science* 4, no. 1 (2009): 24-25.

# ABOUT THE AUTHOR

EDWIN A. LOCKE is Dean's Professor of Leadership and Motivation Emeritus at the R.H. Smith School of Business, University of Maryland. He is a Fellow of the Association for Psychological Science (APS), the American Psychological Association, the Society for Industrial & Organizational Behavior, and the Academy of Management. He is the recipient of the Distinguished Scientific Contribution Award (Society for I/O Psychology), the Lifetime Achievement Award from the Academy of Management (OB Division), the J. M. Cattell Award (APS) and the Distinguished Scientific Contribution Award from the Academy of Management. He, with Gary Latham, has spent over 50 years developing Goal Setting Theory, ranked No. 1 in importance among 73 management theories. He has published over 320 chapters, articles, reviews and notes, and has authored or edited 13 books including (w. Kenner) The Selfish Path to Romance, (w. Latham) New Directions in Goal Setting and Task Performance, and The Prime Movers: Traits of the Great Wealth Creators. He is internationally known for his research on motivation, job satisfaction, leadership, and other topics. He has written numerous articles, chapters and notes about Objectivism and articles which reference Ayn Rand and Leonard Peikoff. His website is: edwinlocke.com.